The Dating Cure

The Prescription for
Ms. Eternal Bachelorette, Ms. All About Me,
Ms. Can't Let Go, and Ms. Matrimony

RHONDA FINDLING, M.A., C.R.C.
Author of *The Commitment Cure*

POLKA DOT
press™

Published by
Adams Media, an F+W Publications Company
57 Littlefield Street, Avon, MA 02322. U.S.A.
www.adamsmedia.com

ISBN: 1-59337-261-2

Printed in Canada.

J I H G F E D C B A

Library of Congress Cataloging-in-Publication Data
Findling, Rhonda.
The dating cure / Rhonda Findling.
p.   cm.
ISBN 1-59337-261-2
1. Dating (Social customs) 2. Single women—Psychology.
3. Man-woman relationships. I. Title.

HQ801.F5521 2005
646.7'7—dc22
2005007445

This publication is designed to provide accurate and authoritative information with
regard to the subject matter covered. It is sold with the understanding that the pub-
lisher is not engaged in rendering legal, accounting, or other professional advice.
If legal advice or other expert assistance is required, the services of a competent professional person should be sought.

—From a *Declaration of Principles* jointly adopted by a
Committee of the American Bar Association and a
Committee of Publishers and Associations

Many of the designations used by manufacturers and sellers to distinguish their prod-
ucts are claimed as trademarks. Where those designations appear in this book and
Adams Media was aware of a trademark claim, the designations have been printed in
initial capital letters.

*This book is available at quantity discounts for bulk purchases.
For information, please call 1-800-872-5627.*

Contents

This book is dedicated to my mother, Anita Weinstein, and my brother, Drew Findling (one of the good guys), whose love, devotion, and support throughout my life has meant so much to me. Here's to the Three Musketeers!

And to the memory of my grandparents
Hyman and Sally Hassenbein

Acknowledgments

I would like to express my appreciation to: Judith Ackerman, Norma Glener, Krupa Surti, Chris Fox, Jodie Clarke, Joyce Hobby, Eddie Green, Susan Gold, Elizabeth Laureano, Gayle Baizer, Simon Yefrem, Sherry Amatenstein, Helen Fisher, Sue Kolod, and Terry Real.

A very special note of gratitude to the following people:

Mel Eisner, who volunteered countless hours of his own time to help me type the majority of the first draft of this book; Alan Levin, who also helped me out with typing while I dictated several chapters over the phone long distance—our friendship throughout the years has been invaluable to me; my editor, Danielle Chiotti, for her great sense of humor, enthusiasm, support, and understanding in addition to her keen editorial skills; my literary agent, Janet Rosen, for her support and belief in my work.

Finally, I'd like to thank all the women who have participated in my Manhattan support group—a wonderful group of cool and amazing women who never fail to inspire me, and all my clients.

Introduction

Dating in the new millennium is a whole new ballgame. Not only do women have to be concerned about their own personal demons, they also have to be mindful of men and their psychological conflicts and problems, as well as vast cultural changes taking place in the age of the Internet. In *The Dating Cure*, I will be addressing how all of these issues contribute to today's dating process, so you can achieve success in your relationship goals. For those of you who have read my books, *Don't Call That Man* and *The Commitment Cure*, you know that I've written primarily about the difficulties many men have with intimacy and commitment. In these books, I've identified a number of behavioral types that frustrate women and discuss the likely origin and developmental patterns.

As a psychotherapist with a lively practice providing counseling to women seeking committed relationships with men, I have also had the opportunity to see firsthand how women contribute to their own problems with men. Sometimes, this negative contribution becomes apparent from the stories they tell of these relationships and the misguided, often counterproductive strategies they employ. Even more directly, they sometimes relate to me in the same dysfunctional way they relate to men, which has given me insight into why they may have difficulties with men.

Women often act in self-sabotaging ways in their relationships with men, including men who might well be available for a committed relationship.

In this book, I will identify and describe seven common female behavior patterns or types that almost invariably destroy relationships with men. They are:

- **Ms. Matrimony.** She's got marriage on the mind. She's dying to get married and will take any single male who has even the smallest possibility of being marriage material. From the first date, she's checking him out and deciding whether or not he's a viable candidate. She also may resort to drastic tactics to get a man to agree to marry her.

- **Ms. Can't Let Go.** She clings to the point of suffocating her man, forcing him to escape just so he can breathe.
- **Ms. Controlling.** She has to be in charge of everything and everyone in her man's life, whether he likes it or not.
- **Ms. Ambivalent.** Does she or doesn't she want this relationship? Nobody knows for sure. Certainly not her man, who usually doesn't stay around long enough to find out.
- **Ms. Eternal Bachelorette.** Mostly happy with her single life, and anyway, there aren't any men around good enough for her.
- **Ms. All About Me.** She's very self-absorbed. Everything is about her, her, and her.
- **Ms. Alienator.** She pushes men away with abrasive behavior that she is often unaware of.

In each of these chapters, I will discuss how women sometimes sabotage relationships with their poor judgment in men, which could be the result of their childhood and other experiences, or just simple desperation. This is especially true for poor Ms. Matrimonial. She puts so much pressure on herself to find a husband that she doesn't want to take a close look at the man she's seeing.

I will also discuss why biology may be the reason women are so compelled by sexy, unavailable men. So, if you are continually attracted to "bad boys," then read on! After an in-depth interview with anthropologist and Rutgers professor Dr. Helen Fisher, I learned that as human beings evolved through the ages certain male types were seen as more desirable than others. Strong, courageous men were highly valued mates in a time when there was no law and order and the family ate only when the male brought home a fresh kill. Even though we no longer depend on a physically strong man to protect us and feed us (in fact, many women are the breadwinners of today's families), we may be genetically predisposed to such men. Sometimes, the man does not have to be especially big and strong to arouse desires in women. This, of course, is not to say that big, strong, or very masculine men are always poor choices. Quite the contrary. Women, because of their genes, sometimes do not look beyond such surface characteristics to the real person underneath, who may or may not be suitable for such reasons as maturity, stability, willingness to be a good partner, trustworthiness, intelligence, education, financial prospects, and so on.

As if women didn't have enough difficulties forming strong relationships with men—now there are cultural factors that make this problem larger. Thanks to the Internet, single available women are even more accessible to men, making it even easier for men to stay uncommitted and continue their fantasy-driven search for the perfect woman. Given this circumstance, the old adage lives on—a good man is even harder to find than ever before!

In addition, I interviewed relationship guru Terry Real, who wrote the acclaimed bestseller *I Don't Want to Talk About It*, a book about men and depression. Terry shared insightful information with me about men and how they relate, and you'll benefit from that information throughout this book. I also cite other experts on male psychology. So, you may come to find that some of your issues with connecting with men are not even under your control.

Don't worry! It's not all bad news! In *The Dating Cure*, I'm also going to provide you with concrete dating advice to help you in your search for a healthy and successful romantic relationship. I'll address both "dating etiquette" and that age-old question that still plagues women even today: "When is the right time to have sex with a man?" Even though many of the cultural circumstances have changed, this is still a large issue for women today. Many a woman still worries about whether having sex with a man too quickly will make him think she is easy, but on the other hand, she is worried that if she waits he may reject her. I will also explore a choice many women are struggling with—whether it's better to hold out for a man you feel passionate love for or to consider compromising on qualities you wanted in a man to increase the certainty of your attaining a committed relationship and/or marriage.

To make sure you get the real deal on how men genuinely think, I've included a round table of five men from ages twenty-nine to fifty-nine who give their opinions on the different prototypes of women. I've also incorporated their feedback about sex, dating, and relationships. They respond to forty questions including: *Why don't men call when they say they will?, When is the best time to have sex with a man?, What makes them attracted to a woman?, What make them want to ask a woman out?* And the best one yet, *What makes them want to marry a woman?*

After reading the responses they gave to these questions, you may never wonder what men are thinking or why they behave the way they do ever again.

Meet the five men:

- *Jerry*, 29, single, restaurant owner
- *Bob*, 40, single, filmmaker
- *Donald*, 31, single, D.C. lobbyist
- *Tom*, 59, married (second marriage, single for five years between marriages), mental health counselor
- *Doug*, 36, single, owner of art transportation company

If you are buying this book to get some help with relationships, you are probably a woman who works on herself, who is serious about improving her life and her relationships. I've made sure to include ways you can work on yourself using programs and writing exercises that will help you become even more aware of any behaviors you may have that sabotage your chances of finding a healthy, loving, gratifying relationship.

In addition to working on your own personal issues, you will also be able to utilize my insights as well as those from several other relationships experts, and the opinions from the round table of men will help you to form your own conclusions on how you want to proceed with your journey of relating to and dating men.

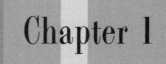

Chapter 1

Ms.
All About Me

Alice, an attractive, impeccably groomed forty-four-year-old owner of a small, high-end antique shop in the Hamptons came to see me when her boyfriend Edmund, a retired schoolteacher, told her he was seriously thinking of ending their relationship. Although she was reluctant to turn to a professional for help, Alice explained that she knew it was time for some objective feedback. She reported that she was very much in love with Edmund, with whom she basically had a happy, satisfying relationship.

Edmund complained that Alice was too preoccupied with herself and always wanted to have things her way. She admitted that she could be hard to get along with and was aware that it probably stemmed back to her being spoiled by her father as a little girl. Alice developed a pattern when she didn't get her way with Edmund. She'd get angry and tell him that he was lucky to have her in his life because she could do much better than him. Edmund would, understandably, get tremendously insulted and tell her that he didn't like being spoken to like that and "didn't appreciate her grandiose attitude." She usually apologized afterward, but would still go back to her familiar pattern of wanting things her way and acting smug when she wasn't gratified. Recently, Edmond told her he loved her but he just couldn't take her selfishness anymore, and if she couldn't make an effort to compromise more, he wanted to end the relationship.

Although she was an engaging, likable client, Alice would often try to switch sessions around when it was convenient for her and dismiss my cancellation policies. I confronted Alice about my own frustrations with her difficulties in compromising. Although it was hard for Alice to hear my feedback, she also was very invested in not wanting to sabotage what she had with Edmund. She knew he was a good, patient man who had the emotional capacity for a healthy loving relationship.

What Are the Signs of Ms. All About Me?

The following signs are a few of the most common traits of Ms. All About Me:

- Demanding
- Grandiose
- Difficult to get along with
- Superior acting
- Bratty
- Self-absorbed
- Egotistical
- Vain
- Selfish
- Only sees situation from her perspective
- Disinterested in others as separate people with their own needs and circumstances

Narcissism and Ms. All About Me

It's normal and healthy to have confidence and self-love. Women who fall into the Ms. All About Me category often project a heightened image of themselves, which may not be based on their true feelings about who they really are. Even though they may present themselves with an air of superiority, their grandiosity is really a front for their deep insecurity caused by deep shame and humiliation. Ms. All About Me has a difficult time recognizing the needs of another person. Her needs always come first. Having empathy for others does not come easy for her. Clinically, these behaviors could describe a woman who's narcissistic.

Sandy Hotchkiss, L.C.S.W., beautifully describes people with narcissistic qualities in her book *Why Is It Always About You? Saving Yourself from the Narcissists in Your Life.*

"It's the nature of narcissistic entitlement to see the situation from only one very subjective point of view that says 'My feelings and needs are all that matter and whatever I want I should get.' Mutuality and reciprocity are entirely alien concepts to a narcissist because others exist only to agree, obey, comfort and flatter, in short to anticipate and meet their every need. A typical narcissistic attitude toward another is: "If you cannot make yourself useful in meeting my need you are of no value and will most likely be treated accordingly."

It's important to note, though, that everyone has some narcissism. You need some of these qualities in order to survive emotionally. However, some women's narcissistic behavior goes to the extreme. I know it may seem horrible to think that you may actually have some of the behaviors listed above, but if there is even a chance you fit the description, it's important to be aware of it because it may be standing in the way of your having a relationship with a man who's emotionally healthy, interested, and available.

I've encountered women in my practice who felt victimized and complained when a man left them. However, I, too, may have experienced the woman as hard to get along with and treat, and due to some of her narcissistic characteristics, she would act out with me or in the support group I run. For instance, a Ms. All About Me could be devaluing, act superior, or be difficult to negotiate with and somewhat bratty. She may elicit in me and group members the same feelings she does in men, discouraging others from wanting to engage with her or, at the very worst, causing others to reject her. How then could I demonize the men for abandoning her when I or other women are having the same reactions as the men?

How Do Men See Her?

At this juncture, some women may argue that many men find it intriguing when a woman acts standoffish, grandiose, and hard to get. However, when I discussed the traits of Ms. All About Me with relationship expert

Terry Real, the author of the acclaimed *I Don't Want to Talk About It*, he remarked:

> *Most normal men wouldn't like a grandiose woman for a relationship. Initially, a man may be attracted to her because she's challenging. And he has to win her over . . . but after awhile he grows tired of it. Most emotionally healthy men would be turned off.*

So, it appears grandiose women may get men's attention in the beginning, but it doesn't endure. For further clarification, I interviewed several men who have dated women with the Ms. All About Me characteristics. Here are their reactions:

Very Demanding

Steve was dating Ernestine for a few months. Although he enjoyed her company, he noticed that as their relationship deepened she started to become much more demanding. For example, Ernestine insisted he give her money to help her out with some of her bills since she was struggling financially. He didn't mind at first, rationalizing that he spent a lot of evenings in her apartment. But her demands escalated over time. One night when she was in bed with a cold, Ernestine insisted that he drop what he was doing and come be with her in her apartment. When he said he just couldn't because he needed to be at the restaurant he owned, she wouldn't speak to him for days. Another time when he told her he was playing poker with his buddies, she insisted he drop his plans and accompany her to a party for which she'd received a last-minute invitation. He finally broke up with her because he felt she was too high-maintenance.

Very Self-Absorbed

Hal told me all about his girlfriend Sharon, whom he described as nice and sweet but very preoccupied with herself. She had a good job in Manhattan and was pretty enough to be a model. He explained that when they spoke she always manage to bring the topic of the discussion back to her. "Sharon never seemed really interested in me. It was like I was just there to keep her company. I never felt like a real person with her. I mean that joke you always hear really happened with her on our first date when she said, 'Enough about me. Let's talk about you.' Then she actually asked, 'So, what do you think about me?'"

Very Cold

Roy told me all about his ex-girlfriend Monica. "She was everything I was looking for cause she was gorgeous, which I'm guilty of admitting has always been a priority for me. At first she wouldn't go out with me, but she was sort of edgy and with that cute bod I didn't mind having to jump hoops to win her over. But one thing I have to say was that she wasn't a warm person. When I went through a crisis at my job and almost got fired, she was very cold. Not at all caring about the emotional pain I was going through. And she was pretty cold in bed too. After we had sex she'd want to sleep on the opposite side of the bed. She wasn't affectionate at all."

Bratty

Tomas told me about Linda, a woman he met at his job. At first he enjoyed her company, but as they got to know one another she started acting like "a brat." "One time when I told her I just wasn't in the mood for this chic flick she wanted to see, she had a wicked attitude toward me the rest of the night. The last straw was when I invited her to my mom's sixty-fifth birthday party and she decided last minute that she wanted to stay home and study for an exam for her job instead, which I know she could have done the day before." Embarrassed that the woman he was dating gave him a hard time in front of his family, he broke up with her.

Superior to Others

When Alan, a struggling actor, asked Naomi to meet his friends for a few beers after a rehearsal in an off-off-Broadway play he was cast in, she bluntly told him that she didn't want to hang out with a bunch of actors. She explained that she had an MBA and only hung out with professionals, unlike his friends who were "just waiters waiting for their big break." Alan never called her again.

Only Dates Whom She Considers Superior
(Famous, Rich, or Gorgeous)

Victor, a handsome bartender, told me about Glo, a woman he fell in love with when he was into the club scene in his twenties. Glo was only twenty-three when they met ten years ago. He described her as beautiful and a great dancer. They immediately hooked up and became known as a couple in the club circles. They were seriously thinking about getting engaged when all of a sudden Glo announced that she could only see herself married to a rich man or at least someone famous. She explained that even though she loved him, he just wasn't good enough for her. Vic was devastated, but after an emotional talk Glo decided she didn't want to let him go. Despite the dramatic discussion, Glo started canceling dates with him. He heard through the grapevine that she was seeing rich, older men behind his back. Not wanting to be made a fool of, he sadly ended his relationship with her.

How Does Ms. All About Me Develop Narcissistic Behaviors?

Do you have any of the signs of Ms. All About Me? Do you think you sound like one of the women in these scenarios? If you do and you want to change, you have to look at the root of the problem first. How did you develop your behavior patterns? Here are some reasons you could have narcissistic behaviors.

Your Parents

Your parents were emotionally and/or physically unavailable. All you had was you to depend on. If you had not been so self-focused, you wouldn't have survived. Unfortunately, your old survival mechanisms may not be helping you achieve healthy intimacy with a man now that you are an adult. Or perhaps your parents were too indulgent with you and you got accustomed to always having your own way. Your parents may also have had narcissistic behaviors themselves and you learned from them. In essence, they were your role models.

Your Childhood Was Filled with Painful Events

If you had a lot of emotional pain as a child due to emotional or physical deprivation, neglect, poverty, physical problems, molestation, or a learning disability, you might have developed narcissistic behaviors to protect yourself from experiencing deep pain and humiliation.

It Makes You Feel Less Vulnerable

You're scared of getting hurt as an adult. You've discovered that some narcissistic behaviors, acting grandiose, smug, or overly confident, helps you feel less exposed even if it pushes people away. You'd rather deal with loneliness than feeling vulnerable and exposed.

How Do You Change?

If you have any of narcissistic behaviors, would you like to make some changes? Here are eight proactive ways to change.

Become More Self-Aware

Observe your thoughts and behaviors. Be mindful. Don't just act or say whatever initially comes into your mind. It could be toxic behavior, or at the very least not conducive to healthy relating. Remember the first step in changing is to admit to yourself that there may be a problem. It's uphill after that.

Lorraine complained to me that men "didn't call her after a second date." Knowing instinctively she had some pattern of behavior that was contributing to this problem, she came to see me for therapy. Through our work she became aware that she was very frightened of making herself vulnerable, so she'd act overly confident and smug to compensate for her tremendous fear of rejection. After a couple of dates, when things were starting to get off the ground, she'd tell a prospective boyfriend that she was busy when he asked her out. She thought a man would appreciate her more for her popularity. She also wanted to present herself as casual, as if she didn't care so much, in order to protect herself from getting hurt emotionally. Unfortunately, her plan was backfiring. It seemed that most of the men assumed she just wasn't interested and stopped calling her.

Make an Effort

When you see yourself acting narcissistic, ask yourself why. Are your actions going to accomplish anything? Is it going to help you achieve a successful dating relationship? You may be attached to your familiar behavior, so being different will be hard work. It may feel impossible, but it's not if you're willing to make the effort.

Lorraine decided that she wanted to do something about her behavior and way of thinking because she wanted to be in a successful long-term relationship. She knew what she was doing on her own wasn't working. So she decided to make the time and financial commitment to both individual and group therapy. She also increased the number of men she was meeting by going to more social events and by putting the word out to friends and coworkers to introduce her to any available, unattached men they knew. She got set up on quite a few blind dates. Bottom line, she was going to make a full effort to get into a relationship and be more authentic in her connection rather than use her habitual narcissistic defenses. She was also going to make sure she'd have enough men to try her new behaviors out on.

Take a Good, Hard Look at Your Childhood

Take an inventory of how your parents were. Were they narcissistic? Did they overindulge you? Write out any possible situations, unhealthy role models, feelings of deprivation, or pain from childhood that could be contributing to any behaviors mentioned in the description of Ms. All About Me.

Lorraine knew that her parents were very self-absorbed and not good role models for relating in a healthy manner. Everyone in her family, including her siblings, was pretty much on their own emotionally and had to learn to look out for themselves.

Do a Reality Test with Friends

If you are having difficulties with relationships, you can try asking friends you feel safe with for their feedback when problems with men you're dating arise. Ask them if they think your behaviors are contributing to the problems. You will have to be okay, though, about accepting some criticism.

Lorraine didn't feel comfortable asking her friends about her behavior. However, she was able to get feedback from the members of her therapy group, who were her major support system through this transitional time and emotional growing period. They eventually became her friends.

Try to Really Listen When the Man You're Dating Is Talking

When you're both conversing, try not to cut him off or listen impatiently, drumming your fingers waiting until it's your turn to talk. Be fully present and try to really listen. There's nothing sexier to a man than giving him your complete attention and making him feel like he's the only person in the room (other than yourself). This is the total opposite of Ms. All About Me.

When Lorraine got serious about dating, she began paying more attention to the man instead of focusing so much on her anxiety and feeling vulnerable. Rather than replay her old hard-to-get routine, she thought about his insecurities and how uncomfortable it may have been for him to take the risk to ask her out on a date. Switching the focus to the man helped Lorraine feel much more relaxed, and she actually started having a good time on the dates rather than thinking of them as some horrible chore she had to endure to get a boyfriend.

Try to Think More as a Couple Rather Than as an Individual

If you're with a man whom you really want to work things out with, try to focus on the needs of the couple and the intimacy between the two of you rather than on just yourself.

- Stop trying to always be right.
- Stop making it a priority to get your way.

Be Proactive about Helping Yourself
Don't just talk about it. Do something.

- See a therapist, either group or individual.
- Go to workshops. There are droves of workshops led by gifted leaders rich with information and insight. Twelve-step programs such as CODA (Codependents Anonymous) are also tremendously helpful.
- Read books. Self-help books, psychology books, and memoirs can be tremendous resources in developing self-awareness and insight into your behavior.

In addition to seeing me, Lorraine also read lots of self-help books and went to some workshops where she did some healing work.

Be Open to Change
Be open to looking at yourself and changing some of your narcissistic behavior you're so attached to and may even cling to. Try to be different from the way your parents were and how they raised you. Have an open mind. Change the course of family history.

Lorraine was very open to feedback and change due to her deep desire for a successful relationship with a man. After six months Lorraine was in a relationship with a man she was in love with and who reciprocated her feelings.

How Alice Changed

In one of her therapy sessions, Alice referred to a scene in *Sex and the City* after Miranda gets married. She and her new husband Steve are deciding whether to live in Manhattan or Brooklyn. Miranda loves Manhattan, and even though it's better for Miranda, Steve, and Brady (the new baby) to purchase the big house in Brooklyn, it's a tremendous loss for her. She's having a hard time compromising with Steve and giving up her life in Manhattan.

Steve reminds her that they now are a family with a baby. "It's not all about you anymore, Miranda," Steve tells her. And in a life-transforming "aha" moment, Miranda replies, "I'm really married." She knew then she had to change and not be so selfish in order to be a good wife and mother.

Alice identified with Miranda's difficulty letting go of her familiar self-centered behavior. She thought of Edmund as her family and decided that she, too, wanted to switch her way of thinking and behavior. In therapy, she realized that she might have been repeating her ancient relationship with her daddy, who loved and spoiled her and didn't allow her to develop the inner resources to tolerate frustration and compromise. She decided that it was time to let go of her old ways she related to dear old Dad and have a more mature adult relationship. Now when she wanted her way and felt like emotionally tantrumming with Edmund, she asked for some time to step away. She'd call someone up who knew what she was going through, did some yoga exercises, or took a shower. She and Edmund started to get along much better, which she was very happy about. In her last session with me, she was sporting a big flashy diamond engagement ring that Edmund had given her the night before.

The Men's Round Table Speaks about Ms. All About Me

Bob

A lot of men seem to willingly gravitate toward these narcissistic bores. I am not one of those men. There is a lot more in the world going on besides their tiny, little, insipid dramas. Please, guys, don't encourage a woman like this, no matter how "good-looking" she might appear to be. Getting into a relationship with a woman like this means it will probably ALWAYS be ALL about HER.

Donald

I think the good news is that there's hope for Ms. All About Me. We all are guilty of some narcissistic qualities once in a while. It is a part of life. Think about your job. In the workplace, you are trying your best to do what is best for the enterprise. However, think about the enterprise or relationship. If I was dating a Ms. All About Me and I really liked her, I would probably try to work things out. However, if time went by and it was obvious that she'd never change, time to move on.

Doug

I've dated women like this, usually rich, very beautiful (physically). The relationship would end as soon as the physical attraction and sex became boring/ritual for me because there usually wasn't enough chemistry going on otherwise.

Jerry

Selfish is a big no-no for me. I can't stand selfish women. I want a woman to think about me as much as I think about her. No room for a relationship with a person who can't do that.

Tom

I've met a few women like this but never dated one. They turn almost everyone off with their preoccupation with themselves and utter lack of interest in anyone else. This is a personality disorder and probably very difficult to change, particularly since she sees nothing wrong with herself, just the rest of the world.

Ms. All About Me reminds me somewhat of the Bette Davis character in *Of Human Bondage* by Maugham. When I was a teenager or in my twenties and really suffering a lot from low self-esteem, she would have had me magnetized. Just an occasional token of love would have kept me bonded to her. Later in life and more at peace with myself, I would have seen her more accurately as cold, self-preoccupied, and lacking in any qualities that would make it worth the time and effort to develop a relationship with her.

Chapter 2

Ms. Alienator

Beth, a twenty-seven-year-old elementary school teacher, became aware that whenever she started dating men who appeared to like her initially they tended to stop calling her after a few dates. She came to see me for a consultation to explore why this kept happening. She told me about Max, the last man she was dating who seemed very attracted to her but then lost interest. At first we explored the possibility that he was an Ambivalent Man. However, as our sessions continued, I couldn't help observing that Beth could be very sarcastic, which I found quite off-putting.

Coincidentally, she ran into Max at a workshop for singles at the church they both attended and decided to confront him about his disappearance. Max told Beth that he liked her but experienced her sarcastic barbs as offensive and felt on guard with her. He didn't think he could have a long-term relationship with a woman with that kind of biting sense of humor. Embarrassed and hurt, Beth quickly left the church. She poured out the story of their meeting in her next session with me. I told her that I also experienced her sarcasm in sessions as off-putting. She said that she knew she was very sarcastic but wasn't aware that her sarcasm could result in pushing men away.

Beth is an alienator.

An alienator is a woman who sabotages her chances of being with an available man by unprovoked angry, manipulative, exasperating, or hostile behaviors.

Even though a lot of the intimacy literature describes women as if they were usually victims, I've witnessed women emotionally injure men with their unprovoked anger or critical comments. In my own experience as a therapist, I've encountered women who are hostile, exasperating, and even aggressive toward me, which has resulted in my counting the minutes until I can get away from them. At those moments, I could totally empathize with the men who leave them or don't want to date them. I even wonder how the man stuck it out with her as long as he did. Do you behave in a hostile aggressive manner that can make an available man who's interested in you head for the hills? Read on to learn more.

Are you an Alienator? The following are behaviors that could alienate an available man you're interested in:

- Using sarcasm
- Demeaning him
- Raging at him
- Being cruel to him
- Humiliating him
- Insulting him
- Criticizing him
- Acting nasty
- Being mean-spirited
- Manipulating him
- Overly frustrating him

QUIZ

How do you know you are an Alienator? If you can relate to one of the five behaviors below, then you may be an alienator.

1. You've heard yourself say cruel things to men you date
2. You think it's okay to start yelling at a man you're dating if he deserves it
3. You occasionally make sarcastic comments to men just to be witty
4. You occasionally criticize men you date because you think you're helping them out
5. You have a tendency to devalue men who are very interested in you

How Do Women Acquire Self-Defeating Behaviors?

Ms. Alienator often sabotages relationships because of family history, learned behavior, and unresolved intrapsychic issues. Here are some reasons a woman may act alienating toward a man:

1. **Sometimes she's copying behavior she saw in her home when she was growing up.**

When children watch their parents, they have no way of judging whether behaviors are healthy or inappropriate. They simply observe and learn. This is called modeling and is an automatic response for a child.

Although Beth's father was very supportive and encouraged her in her endeavors, he'd often make sarcastic comments to her and her brother. She grew accustomed to his sarcastic barbs, and after a while she learned to tune him out. Now she realizes she relates to men the way her father related to her.

2. **Some women witnessed their mother criticizing their dad a lot and internalized their mom's devaluing behavior.**

Erica was a step ahead of Beth in that she was aware of her tendency to re-enact her mom's critical behavior toward her dad. Now, as a grown woman, Erica often catches herself picking on men she dates and often alienating them with this behavior.

She explained, "When my mom was the least bit frustrated she'd go after my father. I even remember when we'd go driving as a family, if we got lost in the car my mother would sarcastically sing to my father, "Here we go loopty loo, here we go loopty la." My father would get enraged and I know he felt humiliated." Erica swore to herself that she'd never act like that with a man. But despite her insight and self-awareness, she was surprised to hear herself criticizing her new boyfriend Harold, whom she considered a catch and was scared of losing.

3. **A woman might act hostile to an "available, interested man" because she looks down at him for being too easy and not enough of a challenge.**

She devalues him for being such a pushover. She literally can't tolerate his goodness. Often she'll antagonize him just to instigate an argument.

Jill was still in the throes of being rejected by a man whom she desperately wanted to marry. She started to do the online personals and met Tobias, a social worker. He was very taken with Jill and courted her enthusiastically, even bringing her flowers each time they got together. Jill began to devalue him, mocking him for his emotional dependency on her while they dated. She reported that she found herself found herself starting arguments with him, goading Tobias to fight back. He finally told Jill he didn't want to stay in such a tumultuous relationship and broke up with her.

4. She's a drama queen.

Drama queens need lots of emotional stimulation. They are only satisfied when they have a mixture of stress, chaos, unpredictability, excitement, and rage in their adult relationships. They find an available interested man too "boring," especially if he's not creating ongoing conflicts, problems, and challenges for her. Being with him is just too emotionally flat. She needs to have a "scene" going on for her to feel alive. When a man participates in her drama, she feels more attracted to him. She will often provoke arguments even to the point of emotionally exhausting him.

Sam confided to Barbara on the first date that he was diagnosed with Borderline Personality Disorder. At first Barbara was scared to date someone with a psychiatric disorder, but he had such a great personality she decided she really didn't care. She was even able to endure their horrific arguments whenever Sam got angry at something Barbara said that rubbed him the wrong way. Eventually, Barbara and Sam broke up and she started dating David, an active drug user. Often he disappeared and popped up again when he took a break from serious partying. Whenever Barbara confronted David about his disappearance, they'd end up having a horrific argument just like she did with Sam. In her support group, Barbara was able to remember how her parents were always fighting when she was growing up. She realized that her intensely drama-filled relationships with Sam and David created a dynamic she felt comfortable and familiar with.

5. **Sometimes a woman is downright angry that her available, interested man is not the "bad boy" she couldn't land.**

When an available, interested man is especially nice to her, she gets angry that he's not as cool and sexy as her last man, who was essentially unavailable. She devalues him and acts out her frustration and anger at him for not creating the chemistry she longs for.

Marsha caught herself snapping at her new boyfriend when he took her to Atlantic City.

Her last boyfriend, Nick, was an almost stereotypical sexy, Mr. Smooth Operator. But she left him when she got tired of his Houdini vanishing acts. Marsha met Stan at a Christmas party soon after she left Nick. Stan was very taken with Marsha and treated her like a princess. During a trip to Atlantic City Marsha couldn't stop comparing her new boyfriend to slick Nick. Watching Stan at the craps table, she couldn't stop thinking how nerdy he was in comparison to her sexy ex.

She couldn't deny that she loved Stan's great sense of humor, dependability, and passion for her, but it bothered her that he still didn't turn her on the way Nick did. She couldn't contain her frustration with the whole situation and found herself picking on Stan during the whole trip. She noticed he stopped calling her every night like he used to, and after the way she acted she couldn't really blame him.

6. **Some women have severe anxiety about closeness and will antagonize a man to provoke him to leave them.**

Once he's gone she can be relieved of the anxiety of the intimacy. She may be disconnected from her fear of getting close, so she splits off her feelings and unconsciously pushes the man away with her antagonistic behavior.

My dentist told me that before he got married he was dating a beautiful woman who was intelligent and interesting but had a very nasty streak. Although he was attracted to her and found her exciting, he couldn't tolerate her mean spirit so he broke up with her. When a mutual friend asked him why he left her, he told her about her nasty side. Their mutual friend explained how the woman was a nice woman, but deep down she was scared of closeness due to her traumatic childhood. Although my dentist is a kind, compassionate man, he decided that he didn't want to be the target of her anger. He told their mutual friend that perhaps the woman should go for counseling to resolve her childhood issues.

7. **Some women have terrible tempers and cannot contain their rage.**

They don't know how to process their anger so they displace it, taking it out on anyone who will let them. Some women feel powerful when they express anger, but, unfortunately, it can be totally detrimental when trying to achieve intimacy! A woman's rage can be so explosive that it can shatter her relationship with a man. Besides, it never feels good for anyone to be on the receiving end of anger.

Betty was a beautiful up-and-coming actress in her late twenties who would be considered by most "a catch." She had a difficult time containing her anger ever since she could remember. If something really upset her, it would be difficult for her not to tell the person what she thought and confront them full force. Because of her beauty, she had no difficulty attracting men into her life, but many of them didn't stick around. It wasn't until she met Brandon that she considered her anger a problem. Not only was Brandon a talented, successful film director, but also he was seriously interested in a serious long-term relationship with her, the type of man Betty always dreamed of falling in love with and marrying. But despite her awareness of her good luck, she couldn't stop herself as she blasted Brandon for his not considering her needs one night when they were planning their first Christmas together. He calmed her down, but told her if she ever raged at him again he didn't know if he could take it. Brandon meant a lot to her so she came to see me for a consultation.

8. **Some women are just plain abusive.**

Sometimes women whose parents were abusive toward them while they were growing up act out such internalized behavior with men they are dating. In other words, they can be the perpetrator as well as the victim.

An emotionally abusive mother raised Laurie. What made it worse was that she was an only child and had no brothers or sisters with whom to share the burden. When she started dating in college, she seemed only to choose men who ended up being abusive to her. She noticed if she was with a man who was kind to her that she would turn into the emotional abuser. It wasn't until she started taking psychology courses that she realized she had a self-destructive pattern she needed to work on if she ever wanted to have a healing relationship with a man.

Although some books proclaim that men like bitches and being treated badly, I have found in my clinical studies and years of practice that most mentally healthy men do not like to be treated poorly. They are very aware that there are too many women out there who will treat them well, so they tend not to stick around if a woman is in any way abusive or cruel to them, no matter what "a catch" she may be.

What Can You Do to Diminish Self-Defeating Behaviors?

By using the tips below, you can put an end to self-defeating behaviors that may be keeping you from the relationship you want and deserve:

- You need to start activating an on/off switch between your brain and how you behave.
- You have to take things slower and make healthier choices.
- You need to become more aware of your behavior and not just compulsively act out. You can't always be on automatic.
- You have to reconsider that when you're trying to have successful relationships with people you can just act any old way, because then you're asking for unconditional love, which is unrealistic when you're an adult.

Sarcasm

The next time you're with your available, interested man and find a sarcastic comment on the tip of your tongue, take a moment to ask yourself, *What's the point? To show how clever you are?*

✔ You can demonstrate your intelligence or wit some other way.

Criticism

If you feel the need to criticize your available, interested man, try to contain it and ask yourself what will you accomplish by criticizing him. Do you enjoy being criticized?

✔ If what you want to say is sarcastic, critical, or in any way mean-spirited, it's better not to say it.

Anger and Rage

When you feel yourself getting angry or enraged, take a moment! It's major reality-check time.

✔ Take emotional space and distance to put your feelings and behavior into perspective.

Momentary Emotional Space and Distance

You don't always have to act out your impulse to be angry, critical, or attacking, so here are some steps you can take to contain your feelings and/or destructive behavior from sabotaging a relationship with a man:

1. **Walk away.**

Don't be rejecting or offensive. Just say I have to go outside for a couple of moments—get some fresh air, step away.

Take a moment and do some reality testing. Try to be objective. Ask yourself:

- Is he provoking you or is it your own issues?
- Has he done or said something that most women would be enraged at?

2. **Call someone from your support system.**

When you talk things out you're less likely to act them out. Be aware of your feelings and express it to your support system. Make sure it's someone who's supportive and won't criticize you—someone who can contain your feelings and offer you realistic, healthy feedback. Ask your support person the same questions you ask yourself.

- Are you being provoked by him or is it your own issues?
- Has he done or said something that most women would be enraged at?

3. **Find a soothing symbolic image and hang it up somewhere.**

Look at a picture that's soothing or that represents a time or place when you were in control emotionally, a more peaceful time. Anything that could immediately calm you down.

4. **Listen to your favorite song.**

Have a song you can pop into your portable CD player that could help ground or soothe you.

5. **Meditate.**

Carry a portable CD player with meditation, relaxation, or inspirational tapes you can pop in and play to ground or soothe you.

6. **Read a book.**

Always have at least one book on hand that can inspire you and give you some words of wisdom to soothe you.

7. **Use affirmations.**

Have meditations and affirmations written out on index cards filled with sayings or quotes that can both soothe, inspire, and ground you

8. **Play a musical instrument.**

Are you musically inclined? Sometimes playing music can be very relaxing and a way to express your feelings.

9. **Do something physical.**

Punch a punching bag, go run, kickbox, dance, walk briskly, jump rope, shoot some hoops.

10. **Indulge yourself with some comforting food.**

If you're on a diet you can always reach for some nourishing crunchy snacks, like celery or carrot sticks or chunks of lettuce. How about a crunchy apple? I prefer Godiva chocolate.

Self-Soothing Techniques: Proactive Steps to Diminish Angry Feelings

If you see that you are continually struggling with ongoing anger at men that results in your devaluing, criticizing, or attacking them, then you have to do some continual work on your emotions. Here are some techniques to try in between seeing the man you're dating:

1. **Transmute your anger into creative energy:** Write stories, poems, paint, bake, cook, paint, play a musical instrument, compose a song, garden, design a dress, sew your own clothes, redecorate your apartment. The list is endless!

2. **Physical exercise:** There's no great tension reliever like physical exercise. It gets the endorphins running and releases all that tension. Kickboxing is great. Imagine the man you're angry at and kick! How about a punching bag. Better the punching bag than the man. Or how about bowling or joining a softball team?

3. **Bibliotherapy:** There's nothing like bibliotherapy to give you strength. There's a lot of wisdom in books!

4. **Meditate:** Take a class; get a video. You can do this by yourself and it doesn't cost anything! Go to an ashram. I had a client in my New York support group who flew all the way to India to study with one of the great masters. She was very relaxed when she returned!

5. **Yoga:** Take a class—sometimes you can even hobnob with celebrities if you're in New York or L.A. If you can't get to a class you can always get hold of a video to teach you how to do it.

6. **Massages:** It's a universal truth that there is nothing as relaxing as a massage—it's just about impossible to be angry and get massaged at the same time.

7. **Psychotherapy:** Psychotherapy will help you find out the root of your anger or any self-defeating behaviors you may be struggling with. It's also a place to process and contain your feelings about the men you are dating. If you can afford it, this is the best way to go.

8. **Nutrition:** Vitamins can always help you relax and not get so strung out. Healthy, nutritious foods are important, too. Skip desserts and concentrate on salads, vegetables, fruits, and the like.

9. **Self-care activities:** Do a self-care activity every day. Get a manicure or a pedicure, or get your hair shampooed and blown out. The nurturing physical contact can relax you and be self-soothing.

10. **Doctor visit:** Discuss your issues of anger with a medical doctor. If your anger is too overwhelming, maybe you need to consider medical attention.

Although your natural tendency may be to say whatever is on your mind, regardless of the consequences, it may be a good idea for you to do some self-examination to determine whether these behaviors are self-defeating in achieving your goals for intimacy and relationships.

The Men's Round Table Speaks about Ms. Alienator

Here are five men's reactions to relating to women with alienating behaviors toward men.

Bob

Surprisingly, this type of woman is one of the easiest types to deal with. It's a relief that Alienators are so up-front with their negativity because you realize right away that you can't stand to be in the room with them for more than another minute. There is very little wasted time and energy spent on your part to figure out what an Alienator is all about. My thoughts: Thanks for the warning, lady. Now I'm out of here.

Donald

Never met this type of girl.

Doug

When I was younger, it used to be fun to break the will of this type of woman—it was like a challenge. Now I won't deal with negative, self-destructive behavior like this at all.

Jerry

I think Alienators are very insecure about themselves. They won't let anyone near them so they will prevent themselves from being hurt. A defense mechanism, if I may. I pity a woman like that if I can see beyond her actions.

Tom

I've seen a number of these women, mostly at work. They would have been far too nasty for me to have even thought of dating. When I did encounter them, I assumed they had serious personality issues and avoided them as much as possible. Ms. Alienator needs help.

Chapter 3

Ms.
Matrimony

Margaret came to see me because her third boyfriend in a year had just broken up with her and she was very disheartened.

"He said he was tired of my nagging him about getting married. He actually told me he felt like a sperm donor because I kept telling him I wanted to start a family and I just don't want to waste any time. Look, I know I keep scaring men off with my concern about their ability to legally commit, but I want to have a baby before it's too late. If they don't want to walk down the aisle with me, I don't want to even date them anyway. I'm almost thirty-four. My biological clock is ticking so loud you can hear it in the next room! I'm not ashamed to admit that I want to get MARRIED!"

Margaret is a prime example of Ms. Matrimony.

Are You Ms. Matrimony? Well, Guess What? It's Not So Bad!

At least you're in touch with your longing to get married. However, if your desire for marriage is taking priority over selecting a man who's appropriate, or you're acting so desperate that men don't even want to date you anymore, then maybe it's time to take a serious look at how you're handling your feelings about marriage and dating. Although it's normal to want to find a man to partner with, Ms. Matrimony goes above and beyond that. She fixates on wanting to marry and drives men away with her anxiety. Although there are men who do want to get married, when they experience a woman as less interested in building a relationship and more focused on "landing him," it can be frightening, even for an AIM.

What Are the Signs of <u>Ms.</u> Matrimony?

Here are some behaviors and ways of thinking that will indicate Ms. Matrimony:

- She talks about marriage on the first date and second date and third date . . . Marriage is her main priority, and sometimes she puts it above building a strong relationship.
- She calls all her friends after each date to review every detail and determine whether they think he's ever going to marry her.
- She has extreme anxiety while she's on dates, wondering if he's the one.
- She religiously studies wedding magazines.
- She reads the wedding announcements in newspapers.
- She's consumed with "wanting to get married." She talks, eats, and breathes the subject.
- She'll get involved with any man who wants to marry her, even if he's totally wrong for her.

Why Are You So Anxious to Get Married?

There are ways we think as well as cultural and biological realities that provoke us to be overly anxious about wanting to find a husband. For instance:

- You're getting older and the pickings are getting slimmer from the dating pool. Unfortunately, it's true! It's shown statistically that the older you get, the fewer available men there are. However, since I've been practicing, I've had clients of all ages, from twenty-one to sixty-eight years old, get married.

- Your family is putting pressure on you. Your mother tells you she wants to see grandchildren already. Your father tells you he's worried about you ending up alone. Even your extended family questions you at family gatherings.
- All your family and friends are married. You feel left out and deprived. Holidays wage a hellish reminder of your single state.
- It would be better for your career if you were married. When you go to dinner and work events, all your coworkers are with their spouses. It just looks more politically correct to be married.
- You're sick of dating. You've been dating since you were a teenager and you can't bear it anymore. Just like Charlotte asks in *Sex and the City*: Where is he already?
- Always the bridesmaid. Just like the saying goes. All of your friends are married or are getting married, and you've been in all of their wedding parties. You want to be the one to walk down the aisle.
- The biggie—your biological clock is ticking so loud you're getting an earache. It's not the most comforting news in the world, but it is the truth. I've seen too many women even further reduce their chances of having a family by squandering their time on men who are obviously never going to marry them. Sylvia Ann Hewlett explains in her book *Creating a Life: Professional Women and the Quest for Children* why it's not so bad to be very serious about dating.

According to *Creating a Life* by Sylvia Ann Hewlett, a woman in her early forties has on average a 3 to 5 percent shot at achieving a live birth through standard VF procedures. Not only do women have an extremely hard time getting pregnant at these ages, but also a forty-two to forty-four-year-old woman who gets pregnant faces a 50 to 80 percent chance of losing her baby through miscarriage.

After age forty only 3 to 5 percent of those women who use the newly assisted reproductive technologies actually succeed in having a child—no matter how much they spend, no matter how much they try.

So, Ms. Matrimony, you might be actually doing yourself a favor with your strong intent for husband hunting. However, you've got to stop your anxiety from leaking into your dating and newly developing relationship, or else you'll scare off all the men and you will be living out your fear that you won't get married at all.

How to Be Marriage-Minded Without Being Overbearing

While it's OK to be marriage-minded, it's not OK to be marriage manic. Here are some tips to help you keep up your search without giving up your sanity:

Get to Know Him!

Do not, under any circumstances, bring up marriage on the first two dates. That's only eight hours—you can hold out for that short amount of time!

Shortly after Margaret started therapy with me, she met forty-two-year-old Joel, who was a widower. His wife had passed away three years before, and Joel had gone through a long mourning period. He met Margaret through a friend at a dinner party. Since they were both avid golfers, they enjoyed talking to one another, and Joel asked Margaret out. Because of our work together, Margaret was careful not to start asking him personal questions about marriage right away. After their first date, which was a long, romantic dinner, Joel asked Margaret for a second date. Margaret reported that it wasn't hard to control herself from bringing up the big M questions when she put her mind to it.

Be on the Lookout for Signs of Whether He's Good Husband Material

Be subtle, though. Don't come on like gangbusters, or you risk turning him off.

Signs of Husband Potential

- His life is stable.
- He's truthful.
- He's reliable.
- He's accountable.
- He can hold down a job.
- If he has a child and is divorced, he's committed to his child—he pays child support.
- He's had at least one long-term relationship or marriage.
- He gets along with his mother—or at the very least doesn't hate her.
- He doesn't make any negative comments about marriage to you.

Margaret said that Joel had all the signs of good husband potential. He always called when he said he would. He didn't lie or cancel. He was very responsible and accountable. And most of all, he seemed to have loved his wife and been a good husband, from what he told her.

Stick to the Three-Date Rule

By the third date, it's OK for you to ask him about marriage, but only in general! See what he says. If he says he never wants to get married, cross him off your list. If you're truly looking to get married, it is a waste of your time and energy to date someone who's not at all interested in marriage. Chances are, you're not going to be able to change his mind.

Don't continue to date men who say the following:

- They're not looking for a commitment.
- They're not into monogamy.
- They don't want a future with one woman.

Also:

- If he shows any signs of instability or unreliability, let him go.
- Listen carefully to what he says about his past marriage or relationship. Utilize the information he gives you to decide whether you want to continue investing time in a relationship with him.

Margaret was very happy to hear Joel talk about how much he enjoyed being married and that he wanted to get married again someday.

Is He a Good Prospective Mate for You?

Here are some telltale signs to help you find out:

- Imagine what your life will be like with him.
- If you have children together, can you imagine him being a good dad?
- Can you see him sticking around and taking care of you if you were to get sick?
- Can you see yourself sticking around and taking care of him if he were to get sick?
- Be selective. Don't just go for any man because he'll marry you—you don't want to set yourself up for divorce five years down the line because you never really loved him.

Margaret thought she had really hit the jackpot with Joel. He was marriage-minded and had all the indications of being a candidate for marriage. Her concern was that she didn't know whether she was forcing herself to like Joel because he was such a good prospective mate or because she truly loved him. She was also concerned that he was still in love with his late wife and had not truly gotten over her yet.

How to Lessen Your Anxiety While in Between Dates

Ms. Matrimony often feels anxious between dates, fearing that she's on a time limit, and this can cause her to be pushy about marriage. But there are things you can do to keep you cool during the dating process.

1. **Process your feelings and anxiety with people in your support system.** Hannah had been in the support group I ran for three months when she met Doug. She was absolutely crazy about him, and he appeared to reciprocate her feelings. They started to date pretty regularly. In between dates, she was constantly anxious about whether anything would come of her new and exciting romance. She used the group to express her anxiety and concerns. Everyone gave her support, which seemed to help calm her. During the week, she called the women in the group for extra support.

2. **If your family puts pressure on you, don't hang out with them for a while.** Hannah's sister was very competitive and would always give Hannah the third degree about the men she dated. Not wanting to add any fuel to her already anxious state, she decided not to tell Hannah about Doug until things were serious. Although she talked to her sister if she called, Hannah didn't initiate any phone calls to her.

3. **If any women friends are throwing their marital bliss in your face, stay clear of them if possible.**

4. **Stop compulsively reading wedding magazines—at least until you're engaged.** Hannah canceled her subscription to *Bride* magazine. (Yes, she really had one!)

5. **Keep meeting lots of men.** Don't get too focused on one man unless he makes a commitment to you. Hannah forced herself to go out on other dates while she was developing her relationship with Doug.

Don't Idealize Marriage

Although marriage is your goal, still keep in mind that there are a lot of people who are married and miserable. With a 60 percent divorce rate, it's not the be-all, end-all. Married couples with kids, the unit that made up nearly every residence a century ago, now total just 25 percent, with the numbers projected to drop to 20 percent by 2010, according to the Census Bureau. The nuclear family is now a minority. By 2010, a single person will inhabit an estimated 30 percent of homes. You don't even need a husband to have children with anymore. Bottom line is you can still have a full life and be single.

How to Keep Things Moving

Your dating relationship has progressed into a full-blown relationship. Here are some tips for moving things along:

Take Him Out

Bring him to gatherings with seemingly happily married couples or go on double dates with them. Maybe their bliss will rub off on him as something to strive for.

Hannah found out that Doug's best friend was married, so she encouraged him to set up double dates with them. After they'd get together, Hannah would point out how content the couple seemed, especially since Doug's best friend's wife was pregnant, and they did appear excited and happy. Doug was very receptive to Hannah's comments and even agreed with her observations.

Take Your Time

Don't always focus on whether he's going to marry you. Use the time you're dating to determine whether he is emotionally healthy and has the capacity for a long-term relationship. You don't want to achieve your goal of walking down the aisle and realize you married the wrong man.

Is He Husband Material?

Here are some important signs to look for:

- He's not physically or emotionally abusive.
- He validates your feelings.
- He's open to looking at his own emotional issues.
- He doesn't ignore you when he's with you.
- He listens to you when you're talking to him.
- He listens to you when you express your feelings.
- He's respectful of you.
- He doesn't humiliate or dismiss you when you talk or express your feelings.

Watch for Signs That He's Committed

If things are going well while you're dating, you'll start to see signs that he's committed to you:

- He sees you on weekends.
- He eventually sees you during the week in addition to weekends.
- He introduces you to his family.
- You go on vacations together.
- He invites you to work-related social functions.
- He asks for the key to your apartment or gives you the key to his.

After four months, Hannah and Doug saw each other every weekend and during the week. They were making plans to go on a trip to Hawaii together for Christmas.

How to Push Things Along Without Looking Desperate

You've been with him for a year now and things are going well. Marriage is on your mind, but you don't want to seem too pushy. How can you move things along?

In your mind, have boundaries and limits about how long you'll date without a commitment of impending marriage (or engagement) from him. Having limits and boundaries helps you to feel less anxious because you aren't powerless in the situation with him. You have some control over your future life. This way, it's not all in his hands.

Don't Keep Nagging Him about Commitment

Just set certain times to have discussions about the subject. The first major discussion should be when you've been dating ten months. The less you discuss commitment, the more viable and credible you sound when you do set boundaries and limits. In between the discussions, try to just work on the relationship. Express your anxiety to the people in your support system. Expressing or acting out your anxiety with him may cause him to distance himself or feel anxious as well.

Discussion Time

After you've been dating ten months and you're not engaged, tell him that you need to know where the relationship is going.

- Remember! Sometimes you have to be able to gamble losing the relationship in order to get the commitment and/or marriage.
- Explain to him that you'd like to get married and have a family and you need to know whether he has such plans with you in the near future.

After the Discussion

If, after the discussion, he still doesn't want to commit, you have a choice to make. You can choose to stay with him without assurance of engagement or marriage, or you can tell him that he's not able to meet your needs and that you need to end the relationship. Don't treat this like an ultimatum! You're not giving him an ultimatum—you're simply looking for a man who can fulfill your needs. If you're happy with him and the way the relationship is going, perhaps you won't feel the need to get married like you once did. Or maybe you're ready to move on and find a man whose goals are in line with yours.

If you decide to break up with him, staying friends with him is not even an option. If he can't decide whether he loves you enough to marry you, then you shouldn't bestow him with the gift of your friendship. It's unfair to you and exploitative on his part.

If he decides he wants to get back together, only go back to him if he's agrees to get engaged. It's not manipulative. You just don't want to waste any more of your precious time. Because every moment that you stay with a man who you know is not going marry you, the clock keeps ticking. As the saying goes, Father Time waits for no one. Don't let these euphemisms make you anxious, but let them make you more disciplined and intent in your choices of men and how you spend your time.

When Hannah and Doug were dating ten months, she asked him where he thought the relationship was going. Doug said he just didn't think he was ready for marriage. Hannah explained to him that she was getting older and wanted to have a family some day and that she didn't want to invest more than a year in a relationship with a man who didn't know if he wanted to marry her. Doug said he understood. When it was their year anniversary, Doug said he still wasn't ready for marriage and didn't know when he would be. Although it was excruciatingly hard for Hannah, she broke up with Doug. It took her months to get over him, and with the help of the support group and her friends, she didn't call him. She mourned and grieved the loss of him. Eight months later Doug called her and wanted to talk. Part of Hannah wanted desperately to get back with Doug under any terms. She had been dating again and couldn't meet anyone she liked as much as Doug. But when she met with Doug, she was determined not to stay friends or go back to him unless he changed, no matter how much she still loved and missed him. But she was willing to take the risk and hear what he had to say.

She was relieved when, at the start of their date, Doug said that he had come to realize by her absence that he did indeed love her. He wanted to know if she wanted to get back together. Although her instinct was to jump back into his arms, she told him she would only get back with him if they were to get engaged. Doug paid the check, took Hannah's hand, and asked her to come along with him—he had a surprise for her. Hannah decided to give him the benefit of the doubt when she accompanied him to a taxi. She thought she was in a dream when she heard Doug tell the cabdriver to take them to Canal Street, an area in New York City well known for its famous jewelry exchange. When they got out, he took Hannah to the diamond counter and told her how much he could afford to spend. Together they picked out a ring.

Margaret didn't have to do all this work with Joel. After six months, he asked her to marry him. It was interesting that despite Margaret's deep longing for marriage she realized that she liked Joel immensely but didn't love him. She was afraid that she might end up unhappy and regretful that she married a man just for the sake of getting a husband. She decided that with all her carry-on about having to get married, when push came to shove she just couldn't settle and decided to keep holding out, not just for marriage but for love as well.

The Men's Round Table Speaks about Ms. Matrimony

Bob
Ms. Matrimony is perhaps my worst nightmare. I don't like women who push the marriage card.

Donald
I never met a woman like this so I can't really comment.

Doug
Run like hell—unless you just want someone to have your kids.

When I meet a woman who exhibits these traits, I usually think she has no self-esteem or confidence or real focus. What's going to happen when the shit hits the fan and you're stuck with a stranger that doesn't really care about you?

Jerry

I feel that Ms. Matrimony doesn't have a great sense of self-worth or is not confident. I can understand how a woman of a certain age may feel this way, but the best way to go about it is probably to let a man know firsthand about your outlook on dating and let him know that you are not out to waste time. Never look like you are desperate to get married. Make it look like you are desperate to marry him.

Tom

I never dated anyone whom I felt to be this type. I would have been too scared off. Just dating her would have represented a kind of commitment. Unless a guy is really eager to get married, this type needs to conceal her desire for marriage. Nowadays, of course, with Web personals, marriage-oriented singles don't have to be so circumspect; lots of men also want to get married and identify themselves as such.

I do recall a girl in college who announced to any and all that finding a husband was a top priority while she was in school. She was otherwise a nice enough girl but scared off lots of guys, including me.

Ms. Matrimonial's best chance for finding a suitable man for matrimony—apart from personals—is, I believe, to pursue her nonmatrimonial interests for their own sake: socialize with people she likes to be with; attend events she is interested in; go to places she wants to go to. If she meets a man there, it's because he's interested in the same thing she is, and neither of them has the discomfort of being at a singles event where they are obviously looking for a relationship. (I would absolutely avoid bars—unless she is looking for one-night stands, quite possibly with a married man.)

If she doesn't meet a man there, she enjoyed herself anyway because it's a place or event she would go to for its own sake. She might even meet a woman there who could be a friend. Increasing the size of her social network increases the chances for her to connect with a man. I don't have any figures one way or the other, but I believe that a very substantial percent of all marriages began with an introduction by a friend or relative. That doesn't include accompanying a friend to some social or other event, and meeting someone there.

Chapter 4

Ms. Eternal Bachelorette

Brooke, an attractive thirty-nine-year-old attorney, came to see me because of her struggle with her newfound desire to become a mother. Brooke told me she had three long-term relationships with men in her life, but none of them materialized into a marriage. With a booming private law practice, Brooke had never given much thought or worry about having a family until recently. However, her father's death stirred feelings in her that she had never dealt with before. Brooke was an only child, so she had no nieces or nephew to bond with. A practical and proactive woman, she had begun worrying that if she didn't do something about it soon, she would end up middle-aged with no children in her life. With a beautiful condo in Trump Towers, constant invitations to celebrity-attended cocktail parties, and a packed social calendar, she had always enjoyed her single life.

But lately she started to be concerned because she was turning forty and there were no prospects of a husband or her own family on the horizon. She was economically self-sufficient enough to consider adoption, but despite her fear of loneliness, she was even more afraid of losing her treasured autonomy. Brooke is an Eternal Bachelorette.

Who Is Ms. Eternal Bachelorette?

The polar opposite of Ms. Matrimony, the Eternal Bachelorette is an autonomous, self-sufficient woman who enjoys being single. Despite her lifestyle, she's open to the prospect of love and maybe a partner. However, she's not holding her breath. And while waiting for her soul mate to come along, she enjoys life and lives it to the fullest. Often, she doesn't want to "settle" when it comes to choosing a prospective husband. Despite her desire for romantic love, marriage is not a major priority for her. She takes responsibility for choices that may have contributed to her staying unmarried and doesn't complain about how life has victimized her. She's aware that her selectiveness in the men she has considered getting involved with has possibly caused her to have had fewer available men to pick from.

Signs of Ms. Eternal Bachelorette:

- She can tolerate solitude
- More often than not she has never married
- She likes to be her own person
- She's usually deeply involved in her career or creativity
- She's usually interesting
- Often she's achieved economic independence—she doesn't need a man to pay her bills
- She's usually picky when it comes to men; she doesn't like to "settle"
- She feels empowered by living her own way and doing her own thing

Ms. Eternal Bachelorettes are into the following:

- Adventure
- Self-growth
- Self-awareness
- Financial independence
- Career
- Taking care of themselves

The Three Types of Eternal Bachelorettes (EBs)

There are three main types of EBs. Perhaps the best way to understand each type is to place them in a pop-culture context.

BACHELORETTE #1: THE CARRIE BRADSHAW TYPE (*Sex and the City*)

She enjoys socializing, meeting new men, and having relationships with men. She goes to great parties, meets interesting people, and enjoys her life. Settling down with one man is dull and boring compared to her exciting, glamorous lifestyle. Married women often envy her stimulating life with new people, her adventures, and her freedom to come and go as and with whom she pleases. She lives and works at what she wishes without having to account or compromise with anyone

BACHELORETTE #2: SAMANTHA JONES TYPE (*Sex and the City*)

She enjoys having affairs with men of all types. And she has no real interest in settling down. She is often impulsive and very focused on the here and now. She enjoys her sexual freedom and is not so concerned about long-term relationships (unlike Ms. Matrimonial). She doesn't want to miss out on any romances or sensual experiences that life has to offer her. Despite her provocative lifestyle, she always manages to earn enough money to pay her bills with either a career or job.

BACHELORETTE #3: MARY RICHARDS (*Mary Tyler Moore Show*)

Her independent, single life may be rich and rewarding, but in comparison to the Carrie and Samantha EBs, the Mary Richards style is less glamorous and exciting. Often, she is more absorbed with her career, studies, creativity, building a business, or athletics than her connection to men and romance. She relishes the freedom involved in coming and going as she pleases without any questions asked. She does not view living alone as a hindrance to her happiness, and she, in fact, enjoys having a life that runs just as she wishes.

Why Are More Women Choosing the EB Lifestyle?

The Eternal Bachelorette is becoming more of a popular living style due to the huge number of women staying single. According to *BusinessWeekly* in October 2003, the Census Bureau reports that married couple house-holds have slipped from nearly 80 percent in the 1950s to just 50.7 percent today. The proportion of women ages twenty-five to twenty-nine who have never married has tripled since 1970. Twice as many women choose to be single today as they did twenty years ago.

This sociological phenomenon is partly due to greater finan-cial independence and sexual liberation. Many thanks to our feminist foremothers!

They Love Their Autonomy

As single women age, they often become increasingly successful and more economically self-sufficient. Their self-confidence often blossoms just from the emotional maturity gained through life experience. As a result, however, it often becomes more difficult for her to compromise and subordinate herself to a man and his lifestyle. This course of events then results in her staying single and taking on the lifestyle of an Eternal Bachelorette as opposed to when she was younger and more amenable to merging her life with a man.

They Fear Intimacy

Despite the alluring sexual freedom of Samantha Jones, which could be liberating and joyful, there's also the opposite side of the coin to con-sider—she might be using sex as a form of acting out. Like some of the men I've written about in my other books, she relates to others primarily on a sexual level, causing her to cut herself off from her deeper feelings of love and attachment that could create a lot of anxiety for her. She may have been deeply emotionally injured as a little girl, and if she keeps all her connections with men on a sexual level, she feels that she'll never get hurt like that again.

Also, lots of sexual freedom could represent for her a coping mecha-nism for stress. She could be using the pleasure and physical release of sex as a way to cope with overwhelming feelings and life in general. There's nothing wrong with this type of lifestyle as long as she protects herself. However, this type of Eternal Bachelorette could burn out as she gets older or her beauty starts to fade, making it difficult to attract as many men, which may be just when her needs change and she begins to want something deeper and more permanent.

Lack of Available Men

Some women are just very naturally independent and are therefore innate EBs. Other women, however, turn into EBs later on when they get tired of investing emotional energy into relationships with men. This type of EB may have wished for permanent bonding with a man, but her wishes may have never been fulfilled. As a result, she is no longer as enthusiastic about putting in the time and effort needed to deal with the anxiety or pain that may surface when trying to attain intimacy with a man.

Throughout the years, all three types of EBs may have been doing all the work to try to become as emotionally healthy as possible, making better and healthier choices by going for therapy or reading self-help books. Sometimes, even after the intrapsychic work, when she is no longer seduced or manipulated by ambivalent, emotionally disturbed, and/or unavailable men, this type may still not be able find the man she is looking for. So maybe it's not all because of the woman's poor choices in men or her issues about her inadequate father or her alcoholic/codependent mother or her need for an extreme makeover.

Some of the problem may be that there just aren't enough good men to go around! Although this whole subject will be addressed more in a later chapter, I bring this to the forefront now because the frustration that occurs as a result of a lack of enough suitable and appropriate men can result in a woman's recommitting to herself and her autonomous, single lifestyle, from which she does get a lot of gratification and reciprocity from work, family, friends, interests, building economic power, creativity, etc. Thus she may turn into the Eternal Bachelorette not just as a way to survive, but as a way to thrive.

To validate my point, I cite New York–based psychoanalyst Dr. Janice Lieberman's article "Issues in the Psychoanalytic Treatment of Single Females Over Thirty":

> *Once women reach their late twenties and increasingly as they get older there is a scarcity of suitable men available to them. The shortage of heterosexual men capable of a long commitment like marriage to women over 30 seems to be a fact of reality that is commonly overlooked or even denied by society.*

Psychiatrist and psychoanalyst Dr. Ethel Person also writes in her book *Dreams of Love and Fateful Encounters: The Power of Romantic Passion*:

> *Unlike men, women live in a scarcity economy: there simply aren't enough men to go around. This problem is compounded by the fact that men often consider women less desirable as they grow older . . . . After a certain age women know their chances of finding love and sex are greatly reduced.*

I've included these last two powerful statements from two prominent, distinguished psychoanalysts to support my observations that women need to stop shouldering so much responsibility for the difficulty they may be having in finding a partner for marriage. It's possible there's only so much they can do about the situation and, therefore, should make the best of being an Eternal Bachelorette if need be, which may, in reality, be a viable and healthy alternative, as opposed to a lifestyle for a woman with severe intimacy issues.

The Realities of Being an Eternal Bachelorette

Even with the accompanying glamour and stimulation of the Eternal Bachelorette lifestyle, there are practical problems she must often contend with, such as:

- Not having a partner with whom to share financial burdens
- Having to depend on herself alone for all decision making
- Needing to be self-sufficient to survive
- Having concerns about what will happen when she gets older
- Having concerns about that will happen to her if she becomes sick or disabled
- Raising a child without a partner
- Possibly never having children

Making Peace with Her Decision

At some point the EB needs to acknowledge what she may not get or experience in life as a result of her choices. As a result of working through her feelings, she will then have the psychic space to make room for any new decisions on how to change or accept her life the way it is. In other words, she may be able to find alternative ways to meet her needs.

The Grass Always Looks Greener

Bear in mind though that although she may have losses to grieve and contend with, there are also parts of her life she needs to be greatly appreciative of. In other words, regardless of the limitations of the EBs lifestyle, there are many married women who would give their eyeteeth to trade places with an EB. Many women who do have husbands are not happy with the men they snagged when they were younger and the dating pool was much more vast. Now that they are older and more mature they may regret their youthful selections.

In addition, many marriages do not work out. The divorce rate is presently 60 percent. But what's even more disconcerting is that many divorced women face poverty. According to Demie Kurz, author of *For Richer, For Poorer,* an astonishing 39 percent of divorced women with children live in poverty. Twenty percent of divorced women receive some type of welfare income.

Some women who do have children are disappointed with t... .vay their adult children treat them. Their children don't call them or they just simply don't have close relationships. These women often experience remorse for the amount of time and sacrifice they made to motherhood in light of the lack of reciprocity later on.

Another common complaint is that women who are married sometimes regret they didn't develop their work life or creativity and instead devoted their lives to their husbands, perhaps supporting his career. They never laid the groundwork for their own work or the career they had a true passion or calling for, or they did and they took a long break to have children. They envy single women who have thriving, gratifying careers, who can earn their own money, and who are accountable to no man for their success and accomplishments. These women sometimes have to put up with their husbands' behavior, which at times may seem completely intolerable, but they are stuck in a situation due to children, financial dependence, or other entanglements. They don't have the freedom to just pick up and leave the way an EB can.

Making Peace with Yourself Works!

In a few weekend workshops I ran for EBs, the women processed their feelings of deprivation and gratitude for the choices they made as a result of their EB lifestyle. After the women expressed their feelings in an environment in which they felt surrounded by empathic, supportive EBs, the following were some of the dramatic changes that occurred:

- Jenna and Carrie found it inconceivable that they wouldn't get married and redoubled their efforts to find a husband. They figured if Barbara Streisand could find the love of her life in her fifties, they wanted a shot at it, too. (Also take note that Gloria Steinem got married for the first time in her sixties!)
- Maura totally changed careers. When she was younger she purposely decided to become a therapist so she could schedule her clients around her children's schedules. She was now almost forty, unmarried, not dating anyone special, never had children, and couldn't see herself as a single mom. She used the workshop to mourn the loss of the life she imagined she'd live when she was in college. She realized after working these feelings through

that her true dream was to become an actress. So a month after the workshop she quit her social work job and started going on auditions. The last I heard from her she applied and got into the Royal Academy of Dramatic Arts in London. That exciting, new life decision came from accepting that she was an EB and taking full advantage.

- Kim decided she wasn't going to live a complete life without being a mother, so she began taking steps toward adopting a baby on her own. The last I heard she is now the proud mom of a beautiful little girl from China.

- Gina decided she always to pen a novel. She took a leave from her job to go away to a writers' colony and devote all her time to writing.

- Jamie decided to go back to school at night and get her college diploma.

- Kate decided to take her life savings and buy a house. She had been waiting for that special man to come into her life so they could purchase a colonial house they could restore together. She decided not to wait anymore and started house hunting that weekend. She said the process of house hunting and exploring old homes from the 1700s with real estate agents was almost as pleasurable as owning one.

- Meredith, who worked for a bank, put in for a transfer to a London branch and moved across the Pond, which had been her lifelong dream. She had resisted following this opportunity before because she wanted to raise children in the United States, but decided not to keep living her life following that goal, which she finally accepted wasn't even near materializing.

- Laura, who was in her very late fifties and who had never married, decided she was going to live in a house with several women, like *The Golden Girls*. She enjoyed her independence but was concerned about living alone in her senior years.

Celebrating Your Life as an EB

If you've decided that you do enjoy your life as an EB, here are some ways to enhance and enrich the quality of life you already have:

Learn to Take Care of Yourself Financially
Learn all you can about money: how to save, how to invest, how to save for your retirement, how to buy a home for yourself (condo or co-op). Watch the *Suze Orman Show* or read her books.

Work on Extending Your Support Network
You don't have to be isolated. You can have a wide circle of people to depend on and who will be there for you when you need them. Build your own family with people you are close and intimate with. Love is not necessarily gotten and expressed through a husband and your own biological children. Love can be given and received in all sorts of ways.

Have Children in Your Life in Some Capacity
Watching children as they grow and change is a part of the life process and can be vital and healthy to take some part in. Strengthen your relationships with your nieces and nephews, if you are lucky enough to have them. Volunteer to feed motherless infants in orphanages or hospitals. Take in a foster child. Become a mentor or a Big Sister.

Utilize the Time You Spend Alone
Use your time productively. Enhance your career. Follow your passions. Develop parts of you that up until now have been undiscovered. Grandma Moses didn't start painting until she was in her sixties. As long as we are alive and breathing, we always have an opportunity to grow and enhance ourselves.

Take Care of Yourself Physically
Since you are self-supporting, your health is of paramount importance—you have to depend on you. Eat right. Don't take drugs. Try not

to smoke or drink. Your body and immune system are precious commodities. The investment you make in your health now will affect your quality of life later on. As my Grandma Sally used to say, "When you have your health, you have everything."

Accept Your Life as It Is Right Now

Rather than sitting around waiting for your future to happen, live it now! Decorate your apartment the way you want it now. Don't wait until you get married to have the place of your dreams. Take trips, have adventures, explore things you've never dared to. Be grateful for your life just as it is. Be open to surprises. Your life can be as full as you make it.

Whatever Happened to Brooke?

I continued to work with Brooke regarding her deep yearnings for a child. She also attended one of my EB workshops. The reality that there were absolutely no children in her family, in addition to her excellent financial state, weighed heavily on her decision-making.

After much research and deep soul-searching, she decided that she would try to get pregnant through artificial insemination. If the pregnancy took, she felt that it was meant to be. If it didn't take after a few tries, she decided she would adopt overseas, since her age was now preventing her from adopting domestically. She, in fact, did get pregnant on the first try. She is now the mother of a handsome, healthy two-year-old boy. She has no regrets and is considering having a second child on her own again next year. Brooke is an Eternal Bachelorette who chose to make the best of her circumstances and reports she is living a very happy and full life.

The Men's Round Table Speaks about the Eternal Bachelorette

Bob

The "perfect" woman. Her own person. Someone who can be respected as an equal and applauded for her individuality and desire to live life on life's terms. Where the hell is she? I'm waiting patiently.

Doug

Well, she can be great fun—so long as you don't fall for her and expect her to change. If you're the jealous type, forget it—you will be in hell when involved with this type, she's out to have fun with whomever and whenever—you might be her "favorite," but she won't dedicate any-more time to you than for hanging out or when she wants something or is lonely. Her job and life come before anything else.

Jerry

Sounds most appealing to me. She's a challenge. She makes me feel dispensable. But do I really want a woman who doesn't need me and doesn't make me feel needed?

Tom

I remember a woman I met through another woman quite a few years ago. She was, I would judge, in her early forties at the time. She was quite attractive, with a pretty face and a good figure. She talked at length to us about her many men. Most of her descriptions of the relationships she had with them, it seemed to me, revolved around how much money they spent on her, especially in the gifts they purchased for her. Men who, in her eyes, fell short on spending were dismissed as unworthy of her company.

She seemed happy with her life. She had a good job, did not lack for male attention, and did not seem at all eager for marriage. Despite what I considered to be her shallowness and materialism, I found her enjoyable to spend a few hours with. She was quite lively, intelligent, articulate, and, as mentioned, very attractive. I couldn't imagine spending lots of time with a woman like her, unless we had somehow developed a very passionate relationship—a doubtful prospect in view of the state of my finances at the time. I could see, though, how easily she attracted male interest. I would guess that the men she attracted were fairly traditional men, not looking for more than she offered.

Chapter 5

Ms.
Can't Let Go

Mary and Brian met when they were both freshmen in high school. They quickly became lovers and were inseparable until they both graduated from college. When Brian went off to medical school, he started to write to Mary less often. Despite her devastation she wasn't surprised when Brian announced that he wanted to start seeing other people. Although Mary intellectually understood his need to experience relationships with other women, she was still heartbroken.

Mary managed to land a glamorous job as a CPA in a fast-paced publicity firm that had celebrities walking in and out all day long. With a new salary, she was soon able to move into her own apartment in Manhattan. Because of her job, she got invited to lots of openings and events and was always meeting new people, and as a result, she dated often. She got involved in two consecutive relationships, but eventually broke it off with both men because they never made her feel the way that Brian did. She spoke to Brian occasionally, but could tell he was nowhere ready to resume their former exclusive relationship. Wanting to just stop thinking about him, she came to my group to get the support she needed to let go of Brian.

Mary is a woman who can't let go.

As the cliché goes, 'Tis better to have loved and lost than never to have loved at all." Despite these profound truths, loss is and will always be a horrific experience to endure, and it's especially hard for Ms. Can't Let Go. The end of a relationship—the loss of the desired love object means having to experience raw, primitive pain. The problem only intensifies when she can't accept the loss. She stays attached to wanting the man back, deluding herself into thinking it's going to end up happily ever after, no matter how much he's hurt her or disappointed her. She just won't give up the hope of a joyful reunion, regardless of how unrealistic it appears to everyone else. The inability to let go of a man who has rejected or shown her that he has no capacity or intention of having a long-lasting relationship is very self-defeating when she's trying to achieve the relationship of her dreams.

What Are the Signs of Ms. Can't Let Go?

There are many traits associated with Ms. Can't Let Go. Ms. Can't Let Go compounds her struggle with intrapsychic issues, having a difficult time with endings and losses when she is trying to have a relationship with a man. It's important to know if you are Ms. Can't Let Go so that you can address and work on your issues and increase your chances of getting the relationship you want with a man.

Signs of Ms. Can't Let Go

Ms. Can't Let Go may be:

- Insecure
- Bombarded with intrusive thoughts of her ex
- Brooding when she needs to consider problems or make decisions
- Overly preoccupied with thoughts of him
- Anxious
- Burdened with abandonment issues
- Overly analytical or intellectual when coping with pain
- Sensitive
- Clinging to the past
- Likely to have experienced some trauma in her childhood
- Unwilling to let things roll off her shoulders easily
- Very romantic

Why Can't She Just Let Go?

When we form a new relationship, we form a memory trace in our brain. When the relationship ends and we don't see the person anymore, the memory trace starts to erode. That's why we do actually start to forget people when we stop seeing them. The cliché that time heals all wounds is an actual biological reality. When we can't let go and still continue to see the person, the memory trace never gets to erode and we keep staying attached to a person, even when they are no longer bonded to us or reciprocating our feelings.

As human beings we are wired in our brains to be attached to those we love. It's a natural human instinct to want to bond so that we can produce children and our civilization can grow and thrive. When that bond to a person we love is broken, we automatically feel pain. This is a natural process of life.

Idealizing Him

When we fall in love, we often feel that the person we love is larger than life. We idealize him and put him on a pedestal. Strangely enough, this is how we often thought about our parents when we were children, so when we fall in love we tend to revert back to those childlike feelings. This becomes a problem when we hold on to this idealistic image of a man who has either rejected us or cannot sustain a relationship.

When this happens, Ms. Can't Let Go has difficulty moving on because she thinks there will be no other man who can match up to the one she's still idealizing. She believes only he can make her feel validated and happy by bewitching her with his magical powers.

Ellen was dating Ron, a glib, charming, good-looking salesman with a very upbeat personality. She always felt happy when they spent time together. In fact, she had never gotten attached to a man so quickly before. Although she knew he was dating other women, she tolerated it because she didn't want to risk losing him. Besides, the sex was always passionate and intense, unlike anything she'd ever experienced. So, she went along with his schedule, only seeing him on Sundays or during the week but never on Saturday nights. Meeting Larry threw Ellen totally off-guard because he wanted a serious relationship. Although Ellen tried, she just couldn't muster up any romantic feelings for Larry, which she told him point-blank was because she didn't want to string him along. Ron was her ideal man. She knew that no man could ever match up to him and make her feel the way Ron did.

Knocking Him Off the Pedestal

His greatness is really your own projection. The cliché that beauty is in the eyes of the beholder is oftentimes not far off the mark! If you look objectively at men you've idealized in your past, you will probably be able to see that you are the one who projected all of this magnificence onto him.

But consider this—with all his great attributes, he doesn't have the most important one of all: the interest in having a relationship with you or the capacity to have an ongoing consistent relationship or commit. So, all the beauty or humor or glibness or money in the world is pointless if he can't or doesn't want to be in a sustained relationship with you.

You need to hold on to the memory of the pain and frustration he caused you. You need to question yourself—why are you more concerned with his looks or charm when you should be concerned with the frustration, humiliation, and hurt he's causing you?

The reality is that you can meet another man, if you give yourself a chance. Almost every woman I've worked with or known in my personal life always met a new man when she let go of the man she was so emotionally attached to.

Don't Keep Looking Back

Living in the past is a violation of spiritual law! In the Bible, Lot's wife looked back and was turned into a pillar of salt.

The famous metaphysician Florence Scovel-Shinn and the author of the infamous spiritual book *The Game of Life and How to Play It* wrote:

The robbers of time are the past and the future. Man should bless the past and forget it, if it keeps him in bondage, and bless the future knowing it has in store for him endless joys but live fully in the now.

All great spiritual leaders proclaim the importance of focusing on the present. Ruminating about the past you had with him and can't let go of accomplishes nothing. It's often self-torture. Most of us would love to jump into a time machine and redo history now that we know the outcome, but, unfortunately, that's just not how life operates.

Try This "Being in the Present" Exercise

Take an inventory of your life that doesn't include the man you're trying to let go of. You must have a certain amount of physical health if you're sitting or lying down as you read the words I've written. So that means your eyes are working, or if someone is reading it to you, then your ears are doing their job. You're breathing. So that means your lungs are working and your heart is pumping. Your brain is functioning. Think of all the good things you have in your life right now and jot them down. Do you have other people besides "him" who love you and you love back? Parents, children, friends, patients, clients. Pets count, too. Do you have interests or passions besides him? Do you have food to nourish you? For this very moment, aren't you perfectly OK without him? If you were like this all day long, staying only in the present moment and not ruminating about what happened in the past or future with him, you'd be perfectly fine. In fact, I bet if you thought about it, you'd realize that your life is pretty full without him in it.

What if something were to happen to you tomorrow and you didn't have your life anymore? How would it be to know you spend your precious last days here on earth constantly thinking about a man you couldn't let go of? A lot of what seems so important to us turns out to be only a matter of perspective.

Although Mary spent much of her time thinking about Brian, she tried the "Being in the Present" exercise in her therapy group. She realized that she did have a lot of great things going on in her life right that she wasn't giving enough importance too. She had a glamorous job, and she got to meet new and exciting people all the time. Excellent health, parents who were alive and loved her. She began to wonder why she just couldn't get past her attachment to Brian when she had so much in her life.

It's All My Fault!

Taking responsibility for a man's decision to leave her or not come through for her in some way is a typical action of Ms. All About Me. Do you often place the blame entirely on yourself? Do you think he's not accountable at all? Do you think it's all about you and what you did to him?

If you think like this, then you don't want to face the hard, cold reality that no matter what you would have done it would have turned out like this; it's out of your hands. Thinking it was your fault and blaming yourself is another way of not letting go.

Ellen often wondered whether it was her fault that Ron wasn't interested in committing to her. She spent hours running what-if scenarios through her mind—if she were bitchier or if she were prettier, then maybe he wouldn't need other women. She read self-improvement books to see what she was doing wrong. She spoke to her friends for hours, analyzing Ron and what she could do to change him so that he would be less commitment-phobic. She just couldn't accept that this was how he was, and if he wasn't meeting her needs, she had to let him go.

But I Really Said Something Terrible

We're not all perfect and sometimes we can say or do something offensive that could have insulted or upset a man, causing him to get angry with you.

As long as you are "accountable" and "own it," then it usually should be forgivable. So if you're aware that you might have hurt him, then apologize for what you said or did. If he doesn't forgive you, then it's his problem. He may not have the capacity to forgive, which is utterly necessary in order to be in a relationship. He may be so psychologically fragile that if you do one thing wrong, you're out of the game. If that's the case, the relationship will end anyway, because being human you're bound to say something offensive at some point.

Another reason he may not forgive you could be that he's looking for a reason to end the relationship. He wants an out. Rather than taking the responsibility to end the relationship, he'd rather make it look like it was your fault and that you ruined the relationship, which is now irreparable. Don't play into this trap! When people are committed to a relationship, they forgive and overlook many things. Some things that people let go of when they are in love are unbelievable! Look at what you're willing to overlook, and don't torture yourself over his inability to forgive. Accept it, work it through, and move on.

As the brilliant psychoanalyst Dr. Stephen Mitchell wrote in his book *Can Love Last?*:

> *Sometimes we hurt those we love and the damage of the past like time itself is irreversible . . . we consider the consequences of our actions on others and are moved to guilt. There is nothing to be done with these feelings, nothing can be done. We bear them and move on informed and enriched as we encounter our next experiences.*

One evening Ron was getting ready to leave right after having sex with Ellen. Ellen thought it was probably because he had a date with another woman. Unable to contain her anger, she decided to share her analysis of him. After reading many self-help books trying to understand her own behavior, she had come up with her own theories about Ron and his inability to commit to her. Ellen told Ron as he was dressing that he was overly attached to his mother, which caused him to get claustrophobic in a monogamous relationship. She explained that he needed to have more than one woman at a time so that he wouldn't feel so closed in.

Ron got very insulted and stormed out of her apartment. Ellen called him immediately on his cell, but he wouldn't pick up. He never spoke to her again. She struggled with deep regret that she had been so blunt with him. The women in the group supported Ellen, telling her that they agreed with her analysis; he just couldn't handle hearing the truth. They reassured Ellen that Ron had pushed her to the point of exasperation and that she had to stop beating herself up. Ellen worked diligently to stop being angry with herself for what she had said to Ron.

The Most Important Tools of Letting Go

If you're trying to let go of a man, you need to feel the loss of him. It's similar to breaking a bone. It needs time to mend and knit. If you try to treat it as if nothing happened, you'll probably just end up rebreaking it. It needs time to heal and you just have to endure the pain until it subsides. Often when we accept the pain, it just goes away on its own.

However, there is something you can do to transmute the pain of the loss. You can create; use it as a time of rebirth to learn more about yourself. Look at it as a new beginning. A new incarnation. A new journey.

Mourning and Grieving

Remember that in order to let go of a relationship with a man, or even an emotional or sexual connection, you need to mourn and grieve the loss of him. Although it is painful to endure the pain of loss, it is an essential part of the human psychological healing experience. This mourning process includes enduring many feelings: grief, hopelessness, anger, despair, sadness, and yearning. When mourning the loss of a man, you will go through five stages: denial, anger, depression, despair, and acceptance, not necessarily in that order. It is necessary to go through this mourning and grieving process in order for you to let go of the man who got away.

Expressing Your Feelings

When you're mourning and grieving, you need to express all of your feelings: anger, pain, grief, and despair. Just not to him. Express it to people in your support system—your friends, family members, coworkers, or therapist. You need to process these feelings in order to let go and move on.

Ellen continued to talk about her feelings for Ron in the support group. She spoke about her disappointment that he never wanted to be her boyfriend and how he cut her off when she said something he took offense to. She shared the frustration, hurt, and despair she was experiencing now that he was gone.

Stopping the Healing Process

Intellectualizing, overanalyzing, and ruminating are not processing feelings. They are just escape routes that allow you to avoid dealing with the raw pain of losing him. We sometimes may analyze a problem we are having with a man to our friends, picking things apart and dissecting it because we don't want to let go. It's a way of staying attached. All of this rumination is just a way to prevent you from really feeling the loss, a disagreement or rejection, which then prevents you from healing and letting go.

Closure

Another form of not letting go is to keep wondering how to have the perfect closure. If it doesn't end perfectly, you may think you need to go back and fix it. But you must know this—no matter how hard you try, *there is no good closure.* If you keep pursuing closure, you also run the risk that he may not be interested in discussing the relationship anymore. Even if he does want to talk and you get to say all things you've been wanting to tell him, then you have to face the pain of losing him again as you both say goodbye. It's just another contact you need to put closure on, and it can become an endless cycle. Separation is going to hurt and be hard no matter how it's done. Accepting that fact is the only way to let go. Don't go back and try to keep fixing it. You'll just keep retraumatizing yourself and you may never let go.

Desperately wanting Ron to forgive her, Ellen left messages on his voicemail saying that she was sorry and would like to discuss it. When he didn't return her calls, she left more messages explaining that if he couldn't forgive her she'd still like to still speak with him so they could have good closure. Despite her urgent requests, he never returned her calls. His not responding only made her feel worse, which led to her leaving more messages on his voicemail, which he also didn't answer.

I Can't Let Go! He Keeps Contacting Me

A man who keeps contacting you even though he's rejected you, or let you know by his actions or words that he's not interested in a serious long-term relationship, makes it harder to let go of him. A man like this is sending you double messages. He wants you; he doesn't want you. Red light, green light. You're dealing with an Ambivalent Man. It's making you crazy, and in some cases it can even be emotionally abusive. Dealing with this kind of man makes it very hard to let go. So it's better to set firm boundaries with him. He either gives you what you want, or tell him he's not allowed to contact you anymore. With an Ambivalent Man, it often becomes necessary to deal with things in black and white rather than shades of gray. If you want to learn more about dealing with Ambivalent Man, you can read my book *The Commitment Cure*.

Self-Fulfilling Prophecy

If you're having a difficult time letting go, you may be acting out a self-fulfilling prophecy. Think about your past abandonments. Reflect on your childhood. Is your "clinging" a re-enactment of "clinging" to an unavailable parent or sibling who you were rejected by when you were a little girl? If so, you may need to work through this compulsive need to re-enact a dysfunctional situation from when you were younger in order to move on.

Ellen told her therapy group that her mother had left her and her sister when she was only four years old and had moved to another part of the country. Her mother stayed in touch but never sustained a close bond with Ellen or her sister. She reported being raised by her father and her grandmother. She felt that maybe she had abandonment issues because of her mother's absence and lack of interest, which she was now acting out with Ron.

Don't Act Desperate

If you're having a relationship or an affair with a man and you know it's not working out but you just can't let go, at least try not to act desperate. Nothing turns off a man faster than clingy, overly needy behavior. Also work on setting limits and boundaries for yourself. The more you gratify all his demands, the more used and manipulated you will feel. Letting him treat you like a doormat will not get him to become more committed to you, to change, or to like you more.

In fact, the chances of him having more respect for you or wanting you more are increased by your presenting yourself as self-confident and entitled. Spin it around. If a man you were dating acted totally desperate and you could just about walk all over him, wouldn't it turn you off a bit? Don't you feel more drawn to him because he's challenging and edgy?

Ellen knew that Ron wasn't treating her right, but she couldn't let him go, so she went along with whatever he wanted. If he didn't want to pay for dates, she didn't care. If he only wanted to come over to her house or if he never expressed interest in introducing her to his friends, she didn't care. If he dated other women, she went along with it. The relationship was totally on his terms, and she realized now that she had colluded with it.

Not Letting Go

The most destructive way a woman can not let go of a man is by trying to force him to stay with her. This need to hang on to her guy no matter what the cost is dangerous, as it turns the man into an object more than a partner in a relationship. His needs or desires don't count—all she thinks about is how she wants him. The most drastic example of this is in the movie *Fatal Attraction*, when Alex will go to any lengths to hold on to her married lover who dumps her after a night of good sex. When she asks him, "You think you can just ignore me?" every single woman who's ever had casual sex with a man, never to hear from him again, probably silently cheered her on. Unfortunately, Alex got so crazed by her inability to let him go that she turned into a psychotic murderer. While she was stalking him, she didn't even seem to care that she had become repulsive to him. All she knew was that she wanted him and had to have him.

Of course, most women don't turn into murderers when their man wants to leave, and when Ms. Can't Let Go wants to keep her guy, there are myriad ways she may act this out:

- Being manipulative—sleeping with his best friend to get him jealous
- Lying—telling him she's pregnant when she's not
- Stalking—calling his boss or friends, camping out outside his house, following him
- Calling him on the phone repeatedly
- Acting desperate—begging him, groveling
- Making demands on him to see her, to call her regardless of whether he wants to or not
- Inducing guilt—telling him she's going to commit suicide
- Threatening—telling him she'll call his wife or boss

You cannot force people to want you or love you or desire what you desire. You must accept that when he decides it's over for him, you need to then work on your recovery and heal yourself instead of trying to win him back. Knowing how to let go is almost as important as knowing how to love, because if you know you can let go then you know you can always risk falling in love. If things don't work out, as Gloria Gaynor said, "you will survive" no matter what the outcome.

Ellen's constantly leaving messages for Ron was an act of desperation. She realized that she was having a difficult time letting go, but gave herself credit for keeping herself from stalking him or trying to manipulate him. She was aware that she could have acted even more desperate and was glad that she had enough sense of self not to humiliate herself even further. Because of the support of the group, she was able to finally stop leaving him messages, and she began to see Ron's refusal to return her calls as rude and cowardly on his part rather than as just rejecting. It was at this point that she could forgive herself and move on.

Although Mary continued to have deep regret and sadness about the way things turned out with Brian, she managed to go on with her life. She had another relationship with a well-known actor she met through her job. She enjoyed dating him, but saw it wasn't going anywhere and ended it. She was relieved that, after years of working on herself, she finally stopped thinking about Brian and let him go. She went through a phase of "not dating," just enjoying her single life, which she had come to realize was full and good. It was the point at which she really didn't care if she ever ended up in a permanent relationship with a man when she finally, much to her surprise, heard from Brian again, after having completely lost touch with him. He had finished his internship and was interviewing for his residency at several hospitals in New York and Long Island, where they both grew up and went to high school. After not having seen each other for years, they met up at the Rainbow Room and had a glorious, romantic reunion, eating, drinking, and dancing the night away. Brian got a residency at a hospital in New York and moved in with Mary. They are still living together and are now seriously contemplating getting married because they'd like to start a family.

 ## The Men's Round Table Speaks about Ms. Can't Let Go

Bob

In my mind, Ms. Can't Let Go is similar to Ms. Matrimony. She needs a man to define the purpose of her existence. A secure man wants an independent woman who has her own sense of self-worth and will do just fine by herself with or without a man in her life. Only insecure, frightened men enjoy the smothering type (the woman who ultimately takes the place of his mommy).

Donald

I do not meet these types of girls. A simple test I use is to see if she has lots of friends. If she does, odds are that she has a separate life and will not be clingy. Thus I avoid girls with very few friends or hobbies because she could be Ms. Can't Let Go.

Doug

Well, honestly, part of me used to enjoy having a Savior Complex—trying to help these women out and to understand things—but in the long run it never works out. They are ultimately too selfish in that they don't care about or how you really feel or what you want, and there is nothing you can do to change that.

Jerry

Ms. Can't Let Go's actions are a sign of weakness, which we all have in certain situations, but come on, get over it! Why would you want to be where you're not wanted? Have some pride. Some dignity. Let go. You'll feel better after you see the strength you'll gain from letting go.

Tom

I have known women like this almost all my life and so has practically everyone else. I'm not talking about women who lack the financial resources or the money-making skills to permit them to get out and take care of themselves and their children. I am referring to women, married or single, who could safely get out but won't.

One reason for this is that they have to have a man in their life, and the one they've got is the bird in the hand.

Why do they need a man in their life? Perhaps it gives them status as a married woman or a woman with a man. Perhaps they need a man to do man-type jobs around the home. Perhaps they need a man to escort them to movies or restaurants or even to family gatherings. Or maybe their life just does not seem complete without a man in it. As we raise more generations of independent, self-confident women, this type of dependent behavior will no doubt become less common.

And of course, there are the women cast aside by men who can't let go of the relationship. Many of them keep trying to contact the man, to no avail. Others struggle continually against the urge to call, but have difficulty restarting their lives. I've devoted a whole book to such women and treat many of them in private and group therapy sessions. There is no single cause that explains such behavior.

Chapter 6

Ms. Ambivalent

Helen, an attractive forty-seven-year-old doctor, claimed that she enjoyed being single but wanted to have a steady boyfriend. Tired of dead-end relationships, flirting, and dates that never went anywhere, she came to see me for a consultation. She reported that she had spent several years without a man, losing herself in her career but all the while still longing for a relationship.

The final straw came when a coworker introduced her to Don, a successful, widowed business man in his fifties, who was very interested in her. He courted her with romantic dates, including a horse-drawn carriage ride in Central Park followed by an evening of dining and dancing. Helen enjoyed her time with Don, even telling her friends that she felt like a teenager again. Yet Helen began taking on extra hours at the hospital, which caused her to have to cancel dates with him. When he stopped calling her, she rationalized that he wasn't exactly what she was looking for. Reflecting back, Helen realized that she had distanced herself from Don by overscheduling. She regretted her behavior and began feeling lonely again, once again craving intimacy. Helen is Ms. Ambivalent.

Who Is Ms. Ambivalent?

Ms. Ambivalent has conflicted feelings about her relationships with men. She claims to long for a committed, long-term relationship or marriage, yet she primarily gets involved with men who make it very clear in their words and behavior that they don't want commitment. While one part of Ms. Ambivalent yearns for a committed relationship, like Helen did, she often acts out certain behaviors in order to keep herself out of relationships.

She blames men for her single state, because she's not in touch with the parts of herself that don't want to be in a relationship. She also projects her own issues onto men, blaming them so that she doesn't have to take responsibility for the parts of herself that don't want a long-term relationship or marriage. Sometimes, her ambivalence is acted out in other areas of her life.

Signs of Ms. Ambivalent

Are you a Ms. Ambivalent type? If you are, you've probably exhibited one or more of the following behaviors at some point in your relationships:

- You have taken advantage of at least one man who was giving toward you.
- You are ambivalent in other areas of your life, such as career, family, or education.
- Your past partners have found you unreliable.
- You've said things to encourage men, only to disappoint them later.
- You are attracted to and get involved with men who are clearly unavailable.
- You've sabotaged relationships with men who were available and interested in pursuing a relationship with you.
- You put off having a relationship for years even though you claim you want one.
- You're overly selective.
- You often devalue men who are interested in you.
- You stay overly busy with work or hobbies.
- You're a workaholic.

Here is the testimony of a woman who identifies with the Ms. Ambivalent personality and writes about how her own ambivalent qualities have affected her life:

"I am a jack of all trades, master of none. It took me twenty years to get an Associates Degree, and by then I had enough collateral credits to get two degrees. I have had over fifty different jobs and never longer than one year for any of them. I am still broke, all due to lack of consistency, commitment to myself, whatever you want to call it. So doesn't it make sense that Ms. Ambivalent attracts ambivalent men, because according to the laws of the universe you attract what you are."

Practical Reasons for Ms. Ambivalent's Behavior

The following are some reasons for a woman to be ambivalent about having a relationship with a man, which are actually mentally healthy, self-protective, and in her best interest.

- She doesn't want to give up the good life she has created as a single woman. She doesn't want to subordinate herself to a man's lifestyle since her lifestyle is already built up.
- She doesn't want to complicate her life—she thinks that relationships are messy, draining, and time consuming.
- There's no room in her life for a relationship—she already has a full, rewarding life.
- She doesn't want to take the chance of getting disappointed—relationships haven't worked out for her in the past.
- She doesn't want to invest the energy—there are a lot of messed-up men with problems out there.
- She doesn't want to take any more risks, or she doesn't want to make another mistake.

Helen felt she had worked very hard to put herself through medical school and become a doctor. Despite her longing for a relationship, she was very unsure if she wanted to get involved with a man she'd have to change her life for. She was very busy with work that she enjoyed immensely and got a lot of intellectual and emotional gratification from. In fact, in dividing her time among friends, colleagues, patients, conferences, students, and the medical community, Helen found that her life was completely full even without a relationship.

Helen also reported that she had had some bad experiences with men in the past. There was Fred, whom she had gone to med school with. Although they had a passionate relationship, she was devastated to find out that he had slept with a woman who was a mutual friend and colleague. Then, when she was an intern she met Maurice, a nurse she ended up living with. She was horrified to come home one night and find that he had moved all his things out. When he finally got around to calling, Maurice explained that he didn't have the courage to tell her that he needed space, so he figured he'd just up and leave. Her last boyfriend, Sean, told her he couldn't see himself getting married after they dated for two years. Tired of being hurt and disappointed, Helen threw herself into her work, where she felt tremendously appreciated and gratified. When she focused primarily on medicine and her patients, there was no real risk of pain or rejection involved. The only problem was that she wanted very much to be in a relationship with a man.

Emotional Reasons for Ms. Ambivalent's Behavior

Often women are ambivalent because of trauma they experienced in their childhood. If you are Ms. Ambivalent, see if you can relate to any of the following situations.

Her Parents Were Abusive to Each Other

Jill, who openly admits to being ambivalent, explained that she was scared of getting too close to a man because of seeing how unhappy her mom had been married to her father. She described how her father beat her mother on an ongoing basis and the trauma it induced in her. Whenever Jill gets close to a man now, she finds herself distancing herself from him even though part of her longs for intimacy and deep connection.

Her Parents Got Divorced

Jill's parents eventually got a divorce, which she thinks has also contributed to her ambivalence about wanting a relationship. She figures relationships aren't going to work out anyway so why even bother trying.

She Was Abandoned by One or Both Parents

Helen, the doctor I wrote about in the opening scenario, mentioned later in her sessions that her mother walked out on her father when she was a teenager. Although she continued to see her mother pretty regularly, it still left her feeling distrustful of people she became attached to.

She Was Physically or Emotionally Abused as a Child

Dawn knew that she had problems with commitment, which she attributed to her mother abusing her emotionally as a child. She told me how her mother would pick on her and criticize her to no end. Now she doesn't like getting too close to anyone because she thinks she'll be criticized. Unfortunately, a part of her wants desperately to get married and have a family.

She Was Sexually Abused as a Child

Some women who have been sexually abused in childhood have very mixed feelings as adults about becoming close to a man. They may struggle with issues related to trust, sexuality, and intimacy. So, although they may long for a relationship, they may also be turned off to one.

Although Ruth was dating three men, she was unable to commit to any of them. After some self-exploration through books and workshops, she realized that being sexually abused by one of her older brother's friends when she was ten was a major factor in her difficulties with getting into a deep relationship with a man.

Smothering Parent

Some parents may become so enmeshed in their child's life when she's growing up, that they may not allow her to develop her own sense of independence. When the child grows up, this can affect her child's feelings about intimacy.

Joanie, a single mom with a two-year-old, realized she'd seduce men only to dump them when they got too close. She claimed she felt smothered by them even though part of her longed for a relationship. She realized that intimacy with a man made her feel the way she did with her mother who was always "in her business." She described her mother as always looking over her shoulder while she did her homework and asking her about boys when she started to date.

Feelings of Inadequacy

Sometimes ambivalent women are afraid of getting involved because they're struggling with feelings of shame. Afraid of exposing their inadequacies, they avoid relationships even though they may yearn for one.

Eight Ways She Acts Out Her Ambivalence

Often Ms. Ambivalent doesn't feel her ambivalence but acts it out with her behaviors and choices, which is a result of her inner conflict about wanting a relationship with a man that endures.

Sabotaging Relationships

Ms. Ambivalent will often unconsciously push available men away, provoking them to break up with her or just not call her.

Dawn acted out her ambivalence by distancing herself from men she was dating. She wouldn't return their phone calls or she'd be late. When Bob, a teacher she had been seeing, proposed to her, she was initially thrilled. Later she found herself overly critical of him, the way her mother was to her. She couldn't seem to control the emotionally abusive remarks she made to him. They broke up before they even had a chance to plan the wedding.

Not Dating

Ms. Ambivalent also acts out her ambivalence by isolating herself and staying away from men. She may cocoon at home, or she may work extra-long hours to avoid dating, even though she claims she wants to meet men.

Sometimes Dawn would go through long stretches when she wouldn't date at all. Not wanting to deal with deep feelings, she would throw herself into her work and avoid social engagements unless it had something to do with her career. Although she craved intimacy, she enjoyed not having to struggle with any emotions connecting her to her painful childhood.

Devaluing Men

Ms. Ambivalent often has unrealistic expectations of finding perfection in a man.

When Dawn did date, she'd often criticize the men to her friends, even making fun of them. If they were good-looking, she thought they didn't dress well or weren't bright enough. If they were intelligent, she'd tell her friends they didn't earn enough money or they weren't successful enough. She always managed to find something wrong with them.

Getting Involved with Unavailable Men

When Ms. Ambivalent does become involved with a man, she is often attracted to men who are largely unavailable—they don't want a commitment or they are married.

Dawn seemed to be most attracted to and most compatible with unavailable men. When things didn't work out, she'd blame the demise of the relationship on the man rather than on her ambivalence and struggle with her conflicts. Her last two boyfriends were married. The man she is currently dating already announced that he doesn't believe in long-term relationships and likes to always have his options open.

Constructing Boundaries

As a protective mechanism, Ms. Ambivalent will often set boundaries that drive available, interested men away.

When Helen (the doctor) dates, she immediately starts setting limits and boundaries by explaining how busy she is with her medical practice, letting men know right away that she is often unavailable. Unfortunately, she constructs so many boundaries that she causes some men to quickly lose interest.

Choosing "Backdoor Men"

Sometimes Ms. Ambivalent will get involved with a "Backdoor Man," a man she is very sexually attracted to but is embarrassed of, so much so that she would never even introduce him to her family, coworkers, or friends. She usually feels he is below her socially, culturally, economically, and/or intellectually. By choosing a man who is completely inappropriate for her, she always has a built-in reason to leave him. She claims she longs for a connection with a man, but chooses a BDM so that she can always have one foot out the door.

Even though Janice, a successful fashion designer, was very sexually attracted to John, a construction worker she had been dating for three months, she knew she'd never bring him to work functions or introduce him to her family.

Janice explained that she met John, whom she described as her Backdoor Man, at a bar three months after he moved to the United States from Poland. He could barely speak English, but she didn't care because the sex was great. She said he was fun to be with and the handsomest man she'd ever dated. But his complete lack of education made it difficult for her to take the relationship seriously.

It was when the holidays started to roll around that Janice was thinking about ending the relationship. All of her girlfriends and female relatives had dates and husbands to bring to Christmas events. She had to go alone because she didn't want to bring John. She came to see me to explore why she was with John, rather than looking for a man she could have a viable relationship with.

Projecting Her Ambivalence onto Men

Often Ms. Ambivalent will select a man who is unavailable and noncommittal so that she can blame the failure of the relationship on the man. By doing this she is projecting her own feelings of ambivalence onto the man she's seeing. If she were to get involved with a man who was completely available, then she'd have to feel and work through the part of her that doesn't want or fears an enduring relationship with a man.

Playing the Seductress

Some Ambivalent Women act out their ambivalence by coming on very seductively to men they are interested in. They are instinctually well skilled in flirting and acting provocative. However, once a relationship starts to solidify, they start to find fault with the man and reject him, or unconsciously provoke him to reject them.

Chuck, an attorney in a large law firm, told me about his relationship with Delores, a paralegal he met at a conference. She seemed to be in awe of him, often gazing at him when he spoke, making him feel like he was the only person in the room that mattered. He found her totally alluring. Chuck was already dating someone and was unsure if he wanted to get involved with Delores, despite his powerful attraction to her.

After the conference was over, Delores started to actively pursue Chuck with phone calls. Unable to resist her seductive efforts, Chuck found himself sexually involved with her. Once they settled into a relationship, Delores became very moody when they spent time together, alternating between demanding and argumentative or quiet and distant. When Chuck found out through a colleague that she was having an affair with another lawyer at his firm, he broke up with her.

Five Steps to Work Through Being Ms. Ambivalent Woman

Here are five steps you can take to help work through your ambivalence, which will also make the messages you are sending out to men clearer and truer rather then a projection of the disowned parts of you that you are not dealing with.

1. Own the two parts of you—the one that wants a relationship and commitment as well as the one that wants independence and autonomy. Try to always be connected to all parts of who you are. The more integrated you are, the more emotionally healthy you are and the better your romantic relationships will be. The more disconnected you are to parts of yourself, the more you will act out in unproductive and self-defeating ways

2. Discuss any ambivalent behavior(s) you might have with a therapist or people in your support system.

3. Work on your ambivalence by yourself through writing, journaling, music, storytelling, painting, drawing, or whatever creative process works for you.

4. Become familiar with your ambivalent behavior patterns.

   a. Recognize that you often choose men who are unavailable so you can blame them for being noncommital or ambivalent.

   b. Recognize that you tend to distance yourself from men who are available and interested in you.

Two Women Who Worked Through Their Ambivalence

Jill, the woman whose parents had an unhappy marriage and eventually divorced, began therapy to work on her relationship issues with men. She had started dating David when she came to see me for her second consultation.

At first, Jill enjoyed the relationship, but she became more anxious as her feelings deepened and she saw David's romantic interest increasing. Jill found herself thinking about all the things that were wrong with him. He was overweight, he didn't earn as much money as she would have preferred, nor was he as funny as she would have liked. She always thought she'd end up with a man who had a washboard stomach and earned six figures a year.

In therapy, she was able to process her disappointment that David couldn't fit her ideal image of the man she'd like to commit to. She discussed her concerns about the lack of stimulation she felt in her stable relationship with David. We discussed her feeling accustomed to a lot of drama and chaos from watching her parents fight all the time. She agreed that being in a safe relationship with David, a man who wasn't provocative and argumentative, was a way for her to distinguish herself and emotionally separate from her parents.

In addition to therapy and talking out her feelings with people in her support system, Jill turned to physical activity (tennis and running) and creativity (she joined a theater group) for healing. Through all these efforts she was able to stop re-enacting her parents' marriage and accept David for who he was, all of which finally allowed her to have a "real" relationship with a man rather holding on to a romantic fantasy.

A lot of credit had to be given to David, who was very emotionally supportive and patient with Jill and her occasional ambivalence. A year after they met, Jill and David moved in together.

Helen, the doctor, used her time in therapy to explore her past relationships with men. Processing the feelings of disappointment and hurt was part of the emotional work she did to resolve the ambivalent behavior she was acting out with men.

In therapy, she was able to connect more with the part of herself that was just not interested in committing to a relationship. She felt deep gratitude for the independent lifestyle she had worked so hard to create. She decided that if a good, supportive man came along, that would only add to her life rather than deplete it, and she prepared to let herself take risks emotionally again. However, until that time, if it was ever to happen again, she felt it would be perfectly fine to continue with her single lifestyle, which she now experienced as full, stimulating, and gratifying.

The Men's Round Table Speaks about Ms. Ambivalent

Bob

Lack of consistency is not always a bad thing. Familiarity often breeds contempt, and spontaneity is sometimes a good thing. However, there is a big difference between a woman who is unpredictable and one who is a flat-out flake. There is a right time and place for every mood. It is the flaky ones who consistently choose the wrong time to be "inconsistent." These women can perhaps be the most frustrating of all types for me. An old adage says that "timing is everything." It may not be everything, but it sure means a hell of a lot sometimes.

Donald

I believe that many qualities of Ms. Ambivalent and Ms. All About Me are the same. It is all about her. All of the time. However, just dealing with an ambivalent person is enough to drive you crazy. The reason is that the relationship has a similar feeling to being on a roller coaster. Up and down; up and down; it keeps going and going; and you have no control. You are just a passenger along for the ride. In order to try to get back on track, you actually have to start setting guidelines because you will never know where you are with this person. People who are ambivalent have a disease that is hard to cure. Men and woman in this category could find themselves as bachelors for life.

Doug

I've dated a few like this—it's usually the case with younger or inexperienced women. Either way, she is someone who is not confident or focused on you or the future of the relationship.

Jerry

There's something enticing about a woman like that. Keeps me on my toes all the time. I like the feeling, but time comes when I realize she isn't for me. Hate to say it, but I do love the thrill of that ride.

Tom

This type definitely has an appeal for certain kinds of men. By constantly blowing hot and cold, she alternates love and kisses with reassurance that he is in no danger of having to make a permanent commitment. Moreover, her recurring cold spells repeatedly renew his license to see other women.

She is in the classic approach–avoid conflict situation: The closer she gets to commitment, the more scared she gets and so she turns cold. The more distance she puts between herself and her man, however, the safer she feels and the more she feels attracted to him. She needs to work on herself to get out of this trap.

Chapter 7

Ms. Controlling

Ellen came to see me for a consultation complaining that her last boyfriend, Tim, told her when they broke up that she was too controlling. In exploring their relationship in her session, Ellen shared how she used to get frustrated with Tim's lack of ambition and often told him what to do to get a promotion.

Eventually, Tim told Ellen to cool it with the advice and telling him how he should live his life. Even after this confrontation, Ellen still couldn't control herself from giving him tips on his career and even how to dress, especially since she felt she was more successful than he was.

Ellen also reported that she always liked to choose the restaurant where she and Tim would dine, which he usually conceded to. This was also an issue she had with girlfriends.

It was an issue that came up during our sessions as well. She would always announce the end of our session a couple of minutes before it was actually over. She explained that she felt comfortable being in control of when the session would end.

It was obvious to me that Ellen was Ms. Controlling!

We all know who Ms. Controlling is. She's the woman who's always telling others what to do, who wants to make all of the decisions, who has to have her way, who must tell you the truth the way she sees it. She's in control.

Ms. Controlling often tries to get her way romantically by getting a man to give in to her wishes. She attempts to control and manipulate men, and she is gratified when they listen to her and do what she wants.

Bottom line is that Ms. Controlling always feels that she has the right to impose her beliefs on the men in her life. But her controlling ways can be upsetting to the men she's dating, because with each statement she's indicating that what he's thinking, behaving, wearing, or doing is wrong and that she is always right. Such controlling behavior can be very offensive, intrusive, and grandiose.

Does any of this description sound familiar to you? Are you Ms. Controlling?

It's very important to be aware if you're exhibiting these behaviors, as Ms. Controlling's ways can make anyone head for the hills—from coworkers to friends and especially men.

While some men may feel comfortable around Ms. Controlling, especially if they had overwhelming and controlling parents, even these experienced men may eventually rebel and take a powder.

Five Signs of Ms. Controlling

There are several ways a woman can act controlling toward men. Here are five different behaviors of Ms. Controlling.

1. Being too bossy
2. Being too judgmental
3. Being self-righteous
4. Being the adviser
5. Being a Ms. Know It All

Reasons for Ms. Controlling's Behavior

The following are circumstances that can cause a woman to act controlling:

- **She doesn't want to be controlled by others.** She may have felt controlled by her parents, older siblings, or caretakers, and she tries to undo her past by controlling people she has relationships with as an adult.

- **Fear of losing a man's love by trying to control him.** A woman may think that by controlling a man she can hold on to him. It's her fear of loss that strongly contributes to her controlling behavior.
- **Role models who were controlling.** Her mother or father may have been controlling, something which she has internalized and is now re-enacting as an adult in her relationships with men.
- **Behaviors she's developed on her own.** Controlling behavior may have helped her to cope, manage, and relate throughout the years as her personality developed and matured. Now her controlling behaviors are not working and may even be sabotaging her relationships with men.

Are You Ms. Controlling?

If you can complete two of more of the following statements, you may be Ms. Controlling:

By being controlling I . . .

- Suffer no consequences, and I always get what I want. There is no consequence to acting controlling with a man.
- Get what I want.
- Can get the man I'm dating to see I'm right.
- Am justified when the man I'm dating has done something wrong.
- Am showing how much I care through my actions and I should be more appreciated.
- Can try to make sure things go the way I want.
- Have more power in preventing myself from getting hurt.

Ms. Controlling in Real Life

In the following pages, you will read several case studies of different types of Ms. Controlling. When reading about these women, see if you can identify with any of the ways they relate to men. Observing the women in these scenarios will give you more insight into yourself and any controlling behaviors you might have.

Bossy

When Sarah asked her boyfriend to come to her office Christmas party, this is how she phrased her request:

"You have to come to my office Christmas party. I know you play poker with your buddies that night, but you have to change your plans and come to my party instead. Everyone's bringing their significant other."

Sarah was aware of how bossy she was and, in fact, reported having been this way for as long as she could remember. After her father's death when she was only twelve, her mother had to go to work full-time. Sarah was barely a teenager when she was put in charge of her two younger brothers.

Sarah claims that she feels comfortable telling the men she dates what to do and can't remember any other way of relating. It was when her current boyfriend told her that he couldn't take her bossiness anymore that she decided to explore the reasons for her behavior.

In addition to trying not to be so bossy, Sarah worked on changing the way she was communicating with men. For example, when she and her boyfriend discussed the Christmas party again, she restated her request. She told him instead, "It would mean so much to me if you'd come to my Christmas party at work. I'm very proud of you and would like everyone to meet you. Besides, it would be hard for me to go to this party alone!"

Judgmental

When Georgia was concerned about her boyfriend's career, she told him, "You need to focus more on having a career, one where you can earn more money and make a living rather than being an artist who will always be poor."

Georgia felt compelled to always share whatever was on her mind with the man she was dating regarding his lifestyle, career, clothes, finances, and whatever else she deemed noteworthy. Anything was up for grabs!

Georgia offered up unsolicited advice constantly because she said she thought her boyfriend would appreciate her help. She learned this method of communicating from her mother and father as a child, watching her mother be very controlling with her father.

Georgia was entrenched in her belief that being judgmental with men was acceptable. However, after being rejected by a number of men for being "too controlling," she thought she might have to consider changing her "mother's ways," which didn't seem to be working for her. Once she remembered experiencing her mother's judgmental remarks to her as intrusive and burdensome, Georgia was then able to start containing her impulse to make judgmental remarks to men. She was able to restate her concerns about her boyfriend's career by saying, "I'm very proud that you're such a talented artist. I hope you'll be able to compensated for your hard work pretty soon."

Self-Righteous

Liz was concerned that her boyfriend's religious beliefs weren't the same as her own. She said to him: "It's wrong that you don't go to church every Sunday."

Liz had a very strict, moralistic upbringing. But in spite of her strong religious background, she always seemed to get attracted to "bad boys." It was as if she was on a mission to reform all the nonreligious men in New York City.

After joining my support group, Liz realized that she felt threatened by men whom she could not control or "mother." She often worried that men who weren't bad boys would be less interested in her because she had less to offer them. When Liz was able to work through her need to chase bad-boy types, her self-righteous remarks greatly diminished.

Acting superior and self-righteous is a turnoff to most people. Acting moralistic to a man about his lifestyle and/or choices can be experienced as narcissistic and grandiose.

Besides, preaching to bad boys hardly ever turns them around anyway! It often makes them badder.

The following Sunday after joining the support group Liz told her boyfriend, "I find going to church very gratifying. I hope that you can come with me sometime."

Adviser

Allie felt that her boyfriend's father exhibited verbally abusive behaviors toward him during a visit. Afterward, she said to her boyfriend, "You need to tell your father not to talk to you like that."

Allie told me she'd been advising her boyfriends since she started dating as a teenager.

While it's wonderful to be supportive of men, excessive advice giving could make a woman seem as if she's superior to him and become a turnoff.

After some soul-searching, Allie realized that she always gave advice to men she dated so that they'd become completely dependent on her, which was a way for her to ensure they wouldn't leave. But of course this didn't work, and they'd sometimes become resentful of her strong suggestions.

In addition to toning down her advice-giving, Allie worked on her communication style. She decided that she would only offer advice if her boyfriend wanted to hear her opinion. If not she'd keep her counsel to herself.

The next time the situation came up, she asked him, "Would you like my advice?" and left the rest up to him.

Know It All

When Ellen came to see me for a session, she began by saying: "You've got to get a couple of new chairs for the waiting room. These are outdated and will turn potential patients off. You also need better magazines."

You probably remember Ellen from the beginning of this chapter. She had a tendency to speak as if she were the expert on everything, making lots of unsolicited comments to men she dated, from their clothes and their cars to their friends—nothing was off-limits for her. She felt free to give her expert opinion on my office décor right down to the lock on my door. It wasn't until her last boyfriend bluntly confronted her that she was ready to take a look at her behavior.

She worked on not sharing what she was thinking all the time and on changing her self-assessment on knowing everything as if it were her job.

Ellen reported that her parents were very passive and she had developed her know-it-all style completely on her own. In therapy, she was able to acknowledge that her inability to contain her thoughts was obnoxious and she began to make efforts to speak out less. However, we both agreed that it was her self-assuredness, in knowing so much, that helped her in her successful management career, in which more than 200 people reported to her. Over time she worked on channeling her negative thoughts about others and her know-it-all ways to her job, where it was often tremendously appreciated.

Her boyfriend, Tim, was particularly happy with the emotional work Ellen did on herself and they hooked up again. They are still together and presently working on their relationship.

Working on Overcoming Controlling Behavior

Controlling also relates to being judgmental, self-righteous, advising, bossy, and a know-it-all. Filling in the writing exercise will help give you insight into whether parts of your personality are controlling.

EXERCISE

1. Think about all your relationships with men past and present. Remember the times you tried to get them to change their behaviors. Times you told them what to do, gave your unsolicited opinions, and/or bossed them around! Write out your answers to the following questions:

    *   Did you want to make them feel bad?
    *   Did you want to help them?
    *   Did you want them to love you?
    *   Did you want them to admire you?
    *   Were you upset with them?
    *   Were you frustrated with them?
    *   Did you look down on them?

2. Describe as many different incidents as you can in which you attempted to control men you were dating.

3. Describe how it feels to be aware of your controlling behavior.

3. Who in your family was controlling with you?

4. Are there times that you feel more controlling than others?

5. Make a list of what you can do to help yourself not be so controlling.

The Men's Round Table Speaks about Ms. Controlling

Bob

A true neurotic and real turnoff (relationship-wise). These are the type of women that men like to have sex with before they ultimately "kick them to the curb." In my opinion, any man who submits himself to a woman such as this has worse issues than Ms. Controlling herself. Why in the world would anyone who has their act halfway together want to be subjected to a domineering woman like this, or a domineering anyone for that matter? I've always thought that guys who are in to this type of woman were basically weaklings.

Donald

I 86 them. Relationships are built on comprises. You will not always get your way. In fact, if you give in once in a while, the payoff could be rewarding.

Doug

I don't deal with these types, period. Knowing what you want is one thing, but running someone over to get your way is not a relationship. I want a partner, not a boss.

Jerry

I do like a woman with a mind of her own. A woman who can be argumentative. A woman who knows what she wants. But like anything else, too much of anything is no good. Such a woman may be good for a man who doesn't have much self-esteem himself or no opinion of his own. Does she really want that? She should be open-minded enough to listen and be open to change.

Tom

I've met some Ms. Controllings in the past but never went out with any of them. One I know is actually a very giving person, doing lots of favors for people with problems, but the price is willingness to let her run your life or at least listen to her prescriptions and commands without disagreeing with her. She is, of course, never wrong about anything.

Other controllers I have met aren't as decent as this one, and their controlling appears designed to benefit only themselves. I remember a young woman in college telling several of us at a table in the campus coffee shop of getting her boyfriend to do something for her. She then said to one of the young women at the table in a very authoritative manner, "You've got to train them."

From what I've seen, the men who end up with Ms. Controlling are the nicest of guys, although probably a bit dependent. I remember an older woman I knew long ago who remarried in her sixties or seventies. Her husband was as easygoing as a man could be. They drove from New York to Florida one time, and, according to a third party who was in the car, Aunt Sally, I'll call her, instructed her husband on how to manage every turn and every bump in the road for the whole 1,200 miles. "That's it, turn right here, right behind that green car there. OK, this is the road, stay over on the right now because the truck wants to pass, watch out now there's a red light coming up," etc. Aunt Sally, herself, couldn't drive.

It took an extraordinary man to drive that 1,200 miles, let alone stay married to Aunt Sally. I'm sure I couldn't have done it. Both Aunt Sally and her second husband are long gone now. He was definitely a candidate for sainthood. I still think of him driving completely unperturbed while Aunt Sally sent out a steady stream of instructions and warnings.

Chapter 8

How Not to Sabotage Your Relationships with Men

Tip #1: Don't Be So Emotionally Available

In other words, don't make yourself so emotionally available right away. While it's unhealthy to play games with men, it's human nature that when someone is too available (in your face), your desire for them starts to diminish because they are not a challenge. Although there's nothing wrong with calling men when you feel like it, being too available to a man can decrease your chances of having a successful relationship.

For instance, if you just had a great date with a man, wait for him to call you first, no matter how bubbling over with excitement you are. You can show or tell him your positive feelings for him when he's initiated the contact.

Often a man has to experience your absence in order to fantasize about and desire you. If you're too available, he doesn't get an opportunity to miss you and long for you.

Tip #2: Don't Be So Compliant!

When you're dating a man, don't be such a pushover!

If you're too compliant, think about why you're so anxious to please him. Are you afraid he'll reject you if you don't do whatever he wants? Do some soul-searching and try to find out what's at the core of your deep need to please. Here are some other tips to help you overcome your push-over tendencies:

- Have boundaries and limits. If he asks you to do anything you don't want to do, just say no—that's setting a boundary.
- If you set a limit and you get rejected, it means your man can't

accept boundaries. So it's good that he's gone. Let him go—you deserve someone who respects your limits.

- Be assertive and express your needs and desires.
- Be edgy. Being a little on the unpredictable side can be very exciting to a man.

Tip #3: Don't Keep Making the Same Lousy Choices in Men

You'll learn more about making smart choices in men in later chapters, but for now you need to know that if you keep choosing men who are inappropriate and don't have the capacity for a relationship, you're definitely sabotaging your success for healthy relationships.

Tip #4: Stop Blaming It on Yourself

When a man rejects you, whether you've gone on just one date or had a relationship, stop thinking it's because of something you did. Take a step back and realize it's not all about you.

Some women will literally cling to their image of "what a loser" they are, refusing to look at other reasons for a relationship not lasting, blaming the man's lack of interest on their hair, body, weight, job, face, or personality. They focus on their own self-hatred rather than on the man's ambivalent behavior.

So in going forward, part of your work is to look at the whole picture—including the man and his issues—and not just at yourself.

Tip #5: Stop Being Naive!

Sometimes women will know a man is bad news but would rather be in denial or believe that he is miraculously going to change. They don't want to see or accept what's right in front of their eyes.

For instance, the man you're dating only sees you during the week, not on the weekends. Or he doesn't give you his home phone number or address. This could indicate that there's another woman in his life—or it might mean that he's married.

Be sharp. If you ignore your gut and don't deal with the truth now, you'll just have to deal with it later. Then it might be too late because you'll be attached, more vulnerable, and possibly in love.

Tip #6:
Do Not Waste Time on Men with Severe Emotional Problems

Once you recognize that a man has severe emotional problems, run for your life! Emotional problems can include drug addition, alcoholism, or abusive behavior. The following is a list of abusive behaviors:

- He yells at you
- He argues with you
- He lies to you
- He manipulates you
- He says cruel things to you
- He intimidates you
- He threatens you
- He refuses to talk to you as a punishment

You know you've been abused if you regularly experience the following feelings with the man you're dating:

- Powerlessness
- Helplessness
- Humiliation
- Fear
- Degradation
- Shame

If you're being abused, you must acknowledge it. You can't conquer something if you deny its existence.

Tip #7:
Don't Act Out Your Emotional Issues with Men You're Dating

Be conscious and aware of how you relate to the men you're dating. Don't re-enact issues from your past, be it your parents or old boyfriends, with a new man in your life. Try to keep emotions separate from a new relationship. If you're feeling insecure or anxious due to psychological issues you're struggling with, or those that are being stirred up by a man you're dating, try not to act out these feelings. Turn to your support system instead.

Whatever you do, don't do the following:

- Yell
- Be sarcastic
- Be cruel
- Humiliate him
- Insult him
- Criticize him
- Be nasty
- Be mean-spirited
- Hit him
- Push him
- Call him names
- Be judgmental

Instead, here are some suggestions of healthier ways to relate to the men you're dating:

- Treat him as you would like to be treated
- Think about what words come out of your mouth
- Don't just impulsively react

- If you're angry, take a deep breath, step away, go back to the earlier chapters, and make a plan for how to cope with your feelings.
- Don't just blindly repeat your parents' behavior—emotionally separate from them and make different choices about how to handle your relationships with men

Tip #8: Don't Cling

Nothing turns a man off faster than a desperately clingy woman. Usually, women cling because they are afraid of being abandoned. So, if you start panicking at the mere hint of rejection, work through your anxiety about losing him with people in your support system or with your therapist.

Clinging does not make a man more mindful of his relationship with you. If anything, it only makes you look desperate, which often turns men off and causes them to distance themselves further.

Allow him to have his space, and when he does contact you, then you can decide if you want to confront him about the way he relates to you, or if you just want to leave it alone.

Strengthen your emotional muscle regarding your fear of his rejection. When he's not around, work on "you" and making yourself feel more emotionally independent and powerful so that deep down you know you can survive if he does disappear. Next time you won't have to be clingy!

Chapter 9

Dating for Marriage Versus Holding Out for Butterflies

When I heard Carrie Bradshaw on *Sex and the City* say, "Some people are settling down, some are settling, and some people refuse to settle for anything less than butterflies," I felt compelled to write this chapter. The majority of single women whom I see for consultations are struggling with wanting to get married and wanting to hold out for a man they feel terrific chemistry for—nothing less than butterflies.

Sarah, a thirty-six-year-old elementary school teacher, always felt envious around her coworker Louisa. They had lunch together often at the school where they both taught and Louisa would boast about her one-year marriage to Peter. Sarah would listen patiently, wondering why it had been so easy for Louisa to find a man she was attracted to and who was willing to commit to a marriage, while it was such a hard task for her.

Sarah was struggling with the breakup of her and her boyfriend who had decided, after three years of dating, that he wasn't ready to make a long-term commitment. Recently, Sarah had met a man who was very interested in exploring a relationship with her, but she didn't feel that attracted to him. The story of her romantic life. Either they were commitment phobics or they just weren't what she was looking for.

When Sarah met Louisa's husband at the school's Christmas party, she was totally disappointed. He was barely audible, speaking just above a whisper. He also stuttered. During the course of conversation Sarah learned that he hadn't gone to college and worked as a clerk in a hospital. She thought this was interesting since Louisa was an ambitious, professional woman working on her master's degree.

After the party Sarah was no longer envious of Louisa. In fact, she felt almost superior to her in that she still had an opportunity to meet a much more exciting, appropriate man than she felt Louisa had settled for.

Many women today are highly educated and career-minded. Although they long for the companionship of a man, they are not willing to settle for just any man. They are very committed to finding a man who makes them feel "butterflies."

It's been my observation that when women are very committed to getting married, they often don't want to exert the patience, the time, or the enormous energy it may take to wait for their butterfly man. Women who highly prioritize getting married will often compromise on certain qualities they would have liked a man they partnered with to have. Bottom line is being "Sadie, Sadie, married lady" is more important than finding passionate love.

I'll share with you a quick personal story. When I was just about to turn thirty-four, I had a therapist tell me that if I didn't choose someone to marry soon I would end up alone and very depressed. Of course she was married. When I had the occasion to meet her husband, like Sarah from earlier in the chapter, I was very disappointed and surprised by her choice, feeling that she had settled and compromised just to be married. Personally, I think what she told me about my future if I were not to marry was destructive and hurtful. I am presently not married, not depressed, and, in fact, embrace my independent, full, single life.

But needless to say, women who are dating with the priority of marriage in the back of their mind (and who are not willing to wait around for the stomach flip) are not so off-course. According to most statistics and the claims made by many women, there are simply not enough desirable men to go around. Simply put, it's social inflation. Too many women looking for too few men.

In my practice, I've observed that my male clients always seem to have any number of women to pick from. I've known men with prison records (felonies), men on SSD (Social Security Disability for Psychiatric Illness), welfare, and still women are clamoring after them.

I once treated a handsome, thirty-something man with a glamorous career who never seemed to lack for options. He would go out to nightclubs every weekend and meet attractive, sexy, available women who were very interested in dating him. He once told me, "I can't get over the volume of good-looking, high-quality women out there. It's like I'm in a candy store."

So, even though it may seem that a woman might have to consider compromising on some of her standards a little if she is dating with the sole purpose of finding a husband, I'm not idealizing marriage either. Many women I've treated who did walk down the aisle were sadly disappointed. They found that they had the exact same problems as when they were dating.

These women were horrified to find out their coupled life could be filled with boredom, anxiety, sadism, and frustration. They were never told this information in the bridal magazines they read so voraciously. Here is a post on my message board from a woman who married for practical reasons:

"I married someone stable who was nothing like anyone I had ever dated. It was mostly because my biological clock was ticking and I really wanted kids. So I married him, he was a great dad and I had great kids. After fifteen years I left him. I think ultimately he was kind of like the rest of them even though he did not appear to be. He was not at all commitment phobic, but I think he still was unable to get close. I did not care, because I really did not love him; we were so opposite."

Even New York psychoanalyst Dr. Susan Kolod who specializes in women and relationship issues feels that chemistry is an important ingredient when looking for a man. She told me, "With all the wear and tear you have to go to in a relationship, it doesn't seem worth it when you're not excited by the person."

With all this said, there are still very positive things about marriage, which can explain why a woman may not want to risk waiting around for her butterfly man to show . . . if he ever does.

Pros of Being Married

There are many benefits of being married that one just can't dispute. See if any of these perks would make you want to give up waiting for your butterfly man:

- Constant companionship
- Knowing someone is on your side
- A steady sex partner (can't beat that!)
- Someone to take care of you if you get sick
- You're automatically "a family"
- The opportunity to have children
- Someone to share a future with
- No more lonely Saturday nights
- Someone to go on vacations with
- Having two incomes
- Knowing there is someone at home with you that night to talk to, eat dinner with, make love with, or watch a movie with after a hard day at work
- Maintaining an ongoing relationship with a man

Waiting for Butterflies

Now let's look at the realities of choice in staying single while waiting it out for your butterfly man. Keep in mind, however, this means not only finally meeting a man who makes your stomach flip but finding one who reciprocates your feelings.

PROS OF WAITING FOR BUTTERFLIES
- You're free to pursue your career to the fullest extent
- You're free to pursue your passions and interests
- You're free to live where you want
- You're free to do what you want with your money
- You're free to grow and learn more about yourself, take workshops, enroll in clasees
- You're not accountable for anyone except yourself
- You can travel wherever you want, whenever you want
- You don't have to put up with someone else's habits or any behavior you don't want to tolerate
- You don't have to go through a horrible divorce

CONS OF WAITING FOR BUTTERFLIES

- Dating can be traumatic—dating for years, subjecting yourself to all different types of men can be traumatizing. Repetitive rejections and disappointments, having to attach and reattach, can take a toll on a woman's energy, emotional and physical health, and psyche. Although dating is supposed to be a social event, it can also be a horrible experience, causing feelings of humiliation and hopelessness. This is a lot to deal with—and without proper guidance, it can be overwhelming.
- You're really alone! One of the major downfalls of being without a partner is that there is no one immediately there to help you if you should need it—such as when you have an illness, financial difficulties, or just a bad day. Experiences like these may cause single women to second-guess the choices they've made.

There are times when an unattached woman can feel especially lonely. She's had an argument with her boss, she's experienced the death of a family member, or holidays and birthdays might get to seem particularly lonely. If she doesn't have a strong circle of friends, she can also feel isolated.

Shopping-Bag Lady Syndrome

Many single women have a secret fear of ending up a "shopping-bag lady," even if they are successful and doing well financially. It appears to be a universal fear among women that they will end up alone, homeless, and broke. If you say to a room crowded with women that you're concerned about becoming a bag lady in your old age, heads will turn! Over half the women will acknowledge they've had similar thoughts whether married or not, although single women are more fearful. Women struggle with this worry for many reasons, which is completely understandable when you consider that, generally speaking, we've only been self-supporting for that past fifty years or so. I hope that in future generations women will become accustomed to being independent and the syndrome will no longer be a problem.

Crazy Cat-Lady Syndrome

Many single women are scared they are going to end up as "the crazy cat lady," the eccentric old women with tons of cats who never leaves the house. Although women can remain unmarried and still have very gratifying lives filled with love, they still struggle with the shame and fear of being the archetypal "old maid" who never got a man.

Sarah's Story

There are no "right" choices when deciding between settling for marriage and waiting for Mr. Butterfly. Here's what happened to Sarah, the woman from the opening story of this chapter.

Sarah tried different avenues for meeting men over the next three years. Like Carrie Bradshaw, she had lots of stories and experiences, but none of the relationships with men went anywhere. And then, one evening, she attended a cocktail party given by the National Society of Defense Lawyers, where she met David. David, who was thirty-four, had been divorced for a few years, having married right out of college. He and his ex-wife had had different goals and values with respect to having a family: She was sure she didn't want children and David wanted a family more and more as he got older. They separated amicably and were still friends.

It was all pretty simple. They spoke, had some laughs and exchanged business cards. He called her the next day and asked her to dinner. They went out that Saturday night and he paid. After a movie and romantic dinner, they made out in her living room for hours. When he got ready to leave, they made plans for the next Saturday night. No games. A month later they spent the whole night together and made love. He sent her flowers the next day.

Sarah was definitely attracted to David. It wasn't all-consuming or stomach flipping, but the relationship felt real. Her feelings were based less on intense chemistry and more on what was growing between them as they spent time together. She enjoyed his company. He was outgoing, personable, talkative, funny, and good company. He wasn't as handsome, tall, edgy, and stimulating as she usually liked, but his warmth, attentiveness, and consistency, which allowed her to feel tremendously connected and secure, certainly made up for it.

After dating almost a year, David told Sarah that he was in love with her and wanted to marry her. Sarah accepted and they got engaged. One year later Sarah was a married and pregnant with her first child. Although she would have liked to be a first-time mom when she was in her late twenties or very early thirties, Sarah decided that David and the life they now shared had been worth the wait!

Chapter 10

When Is the Right Time to Have Sex?

Sex is always complicated, isn't it? I talk to women every day about sex and relationships, and the most common complaints I hear from women about men are:

"If you sleep with a man right away, he thinks you're too easy and doesn't call you again. If you turn him down, then he feels rejected and doesn't call. You can't win either way."

—Mary, 32, Arkansas

"Once you have sex with a man his ardor starts to cool. He starts to lose interest because the challenge to seduce is over."

—Susan, 29, Florida

One of the most popular questions I get is if there's a right time to have sex with men that ensures you won't get hurt. My initial reaction is, "What's wrong with just expressing your sexuality, even initiating it?" Isn't it joyous and self-empowering to express your desire and passion when you feel like it? Why should we fight the dopamine, norepinephrine, and phenylethylamine that's soaring through our bodies and creating that delicious euphoria? Why shouldn't we just enjoy one of the few free pleasures that life offers us?

As women, aren't we more financially and sexually independent now than we've ever been before? Isn't that what the feminist sexual revolution was all about? To do what we want with our bodies? Why should we forfeit the accomplishments and hard-won rewards that women have fought so hard for?

But then I pause and think of my recent session with Josie.

Josie, an attractive, confident woman from New York City who was fresh out of a divorce, went to a trendy nightclub one evening with a girlfriend. At the club, Josie met Rick, a businessman with Hollywood looks, who immediately asked to buy her a drink. Their discussion moved quickly from their jobs to their spouses. Although Josie was having a great time with Rick, she left early because she had to get up for an early business meeting the next morning.

Rick called a few days later and asked her out. He impressed her by taking her to a hit Broadway show, followed by drinks at a club that had just opened. Josie was very attracted to Rick, and because he spent so much money on the date, she assumed he reciprocated her feelings. She asked him up to her apartment, and before she knew it they were in her bedroom tearing one anothers' clothes off.

Josie woke up the next morning with stars in her eyes. She fixed breakfast for Rick, and after polishing off the omelet, orange juice, and biscuits she had made for him, he kissed her lightly on the lips, and as he was walking out the door, casually said, "Thanks, I had a great time."

After he left, needless to say, Josie never heard from him again.

It took Josie three months to recover from feeling humiliated and used from her experience with Rick. She decided the pleasure wasn't worth all the grief for having sex with a man she barely knew regardless of how "hot" the guy was.

Thinking It Through

Now is a good time to dig deep into your psyche and ask yourself why you want to sexualize your relationship with this man. It's always good to take a moment to reflect and process your feelings before impulsively jumping into a sexual situation.

You can start out by trying to determine what kind of man you're dealing with. This could be done by analyzing a man's "risk factor," which will help you to reduce your chances of having a bad experience like Josie's.

Although you can never predict what a person's going to do, there are obvious red flags you must be mindful of. So, be alert and be honest with yourself when you are trying to determine a man's motives and/or character. It's good to think positively, but in this case a little skepticism and a touch of paranoia might be healthy in trying to protect yourself from getting hurt. Sometimes your instincts can tell you if a man is dangerous and a user. Don't be afraid to go by your gut!

If a guy has a high risk factor, he will most likely demonstrate one or more of the following personality characteristics:

- He's unreliable
- He has lied to you at least once
- He's not punctual
- He's mysterious
- He's elusive
- He calls inconsistently
- He's emotionally and/or physically unavailable
- He acts ambivalent
- What he says doesn't always coincide with his actions

If a guy has a low risk factor, he will most likely demonstrate one or more of the following personality characteristics:

- He's very present
- He's consistent
- He calls often
- He's available
- He's punctual
- He's trustworthy
- His actions match what he tells you

Now that you've determined he's a man you want to have sex with, here are some very important issues to think about.

Casual Sex or a Deep Attachment?
After all, we are all sexual beings, and there are times we may experience "sexual hunger." So, if he turns you on and you just want to have

casual sex, then go for it, girlfriend! But you must accept that this is what it will be and nothing more. If something comes of it, then so be it. But if not, you got your needs met and you won't feel "played." Just remember that gratifying your sexual needs doesn't necessarily guarantee that you're fulfilling your emotional needs. Also, keep in mind that when you have sex the hormone oxytocin is released in your brain, which will make you feel more attached to him and could intensify your casual feelings, so be careful.

If you want to have sex with a man because you feel deeply attracted to him, possibly in love him, and you want a long-term relationship, you may need to have higher standards and wait awhile longer when evaluating whether or not he's a keeper. To lower your chances of getting hurt, it's also important to make sure that he reciprocates your feelings.

Don't Use Sex as an Escape Route

Using sex as an excuse to run away from your problems may not be the greatest reason to sleep with a man. You're better off trying to work through whatever you're struggling with than using sex as a method of escape. Although sex feels good, you'll be right back to your problems when it's over, with possibly more problems because you're now attached to someone who may not be a good choice for you in the long run.

Prepare Yourself for Anxiety

When you have sex with a man, you're taking a big emotional risk, so it's natural that you may feel anxious afterward when you both have to separate and carry on with your daily lives. The unknown is scary after you've taken a big emotional risk, so have friends ready to talk to and activities to do (including work) to keep your mind occupied.

Take Care of Yourself Physically

You can't completely protect yourself emotionally, but you can protect yourself physically by using condoms. The percentage of women getting HIV from heterosexual sex is rising. Don't think you're invulnerable. Don't be in denial. Having unprotected sex is like playing Russian roulette.

Consider Setting Boundaries and Limits

When you're in a sexual situation with a man, know you can stop whenever you want to. This may sound high schoolish, but you don't have to go all the way! You can still be sexual without having intercourse. Perhaps this compromise will help you be more comfortable until you feel ready.

Be Honest

There's nothing wrong with being honest and up-front with a man. Own your truth. Tell him what the deal is before you have sex so there are no misunderstandings later on. For instance, if you know that you are looking for a boyfriend and not a fling, you can tell him that you are not into casual sex; if that's what he's interested in, then it's probably not a good idea for the two of you to hook up. You also have the right to ask him what you need to know to help you make the best choice. For instance, you can ask him if he's seeing anyone else, what he wants from hooking up with you, or if he's looking for a relationship. Listen carefully to what he tells you. If he's honest enough to admit there's no future and it's just for the night, then believe him. Don't play mind games with yourself. Don't be grandiose and think that you're the exception. See how he reacts to what you tell him. After you hear what he comes back with, evaluate whether or not he can meet your needs and then make your final decision.

* WARNING *

When you're trying to determine whether it's emotionally or physically safe to have sex with a man, don't drink or take any drugs. You want to be alert and have a clear mind. If you want to be smart and make the healthiest choices, you don't want anything in your system that will cloud your perception.

After Sex

After you've had sex with a man for the first time, be yourself but hold back a little. Take your cue from how he responds. If you're lucky enough to have sex with a great guy who's telling you how happy he is to be finally hooking up with you and calls you the next day, lucky you! Just enjoy the process. You don't need to read any further.

However, if he acts cold and detached or wants to leave without even cuddling, don't cling to his ankles as he walks out the door. I strongly advise against making a scene. Wait till he leaves, and then you can get crazy and call all your girlfriends. If it makes you feel a little better, you could say something about his distancing behavior, but make sure you sound calm. A little constructive criticism probably won't hurt him. He may need some coaching in this area. Just don't come off as verbally castrating or reprimanding. Remember not to give him the satisfaction of how upset you are. Work out your deep feelings with people in your support system.

If you don't hear from him again, it could be for a number of reasons: He's scared of a relationship, he has a girlfriend, he's married, he just wanted a one-night stand, or he's having an anxiety attack.

If you are looking for a relationship, I don't suggest calling him. If you don't hear from him within a week, he's just not good relationship material, no matter how amazing you thought he was. Instead, grieve and mourn the loss of him and the hope of the possibilities of what you both would have had together. Chalk it up to experience to learn and grow from. I hope the sex was good.

If casual sex is your goal and nothing traumatic happened, you could say something like, "I had a great time; let's do it again." Only suggest this if you can emotionally handle risking his not responding favorably.

No matter how things pan out in either case, remember you are not a victim; you had a choice. Take it like the great woman you are.

So, when is the right time to have sex with a man?

I think anywhere from two dates until two months is a reasonable amount of time to wait to have sex with a man. Whether it's the first date or two months later is individual. It depends on your comfort level.

Although I don't think it's a good idea to have sex when you're not ready just to please a man, I also think it's not a good idea to purposely put off sex just to see how long a man will wait. Either having sex to "get" the guy or not having sex to "test" the guy is manipulative and an expression of a woman's own psychological issues, which is not based on authentic intimacy and relationship. The sad truth is that most men in the American culture who are capable of a relationship, whom you and other women find sexually attractive, will probably have a difficult time waiting longer than three months. So if you're going to make him wait four months to see if he really cares, his feelings of frustration, deprivation, and rejection will probably cause him to leave you anyway. The nicest guy can feel insulted even though your reason to wait has nothing to do with his desirability. If you explain that you need to wait because of being hurt by men from your past, don't expect a man to be so generous and take the hit for your past insensitive boyfriends; it's just not realistic. The only men who could tolerate waiting four months or longer are probably gay, sexually dysfunctional, or afraid of intimacy, or they just enjoy being with women who are frustrating or withholding.

If a woman needs to make a man wait longer than three months, she may be struggling with her own sexual issues. I think she should look into why it takes her so long to feel comfortable having sex with a man. Is she distrustful of men? Did a man hurt her?

Here's a list of the pros and cons of waiting to have sex with a man to help you determine when the best time is for you.

Cons of Waiting
Waiting at least three to five dates until two months is reasonable. If you wait and he still leaves after you become sexual, it will be even more devastating because you're more attached to him.

- By having sex with him, you get to know him in an intimate way that will help you to determine if you want to keep seeing him.
- If it's meant to be, it'll work out no matter when you have sex, so why bother waiting.

- Be true to yourself, and if you're really into him, then go for it—why put up pretenses?
- It feels good to make love, connect to a man, and have intimacy.
- If he's going to abandon you after sex, you might as well sleep with him, have a good time, and just get it over with.
- Enjoy your life! We only have a short time on this earth—who knows what'll happen tomorrow.
- It will accelerate the relationship and intensify the bonding.

Pros of Waiting

Keep in mind, waiting at least two to three dates until two months is reasonable.

- The sex could be better when you finally do get together because you have the foundation of a relationship, which can intensify the passion.
- You get to know the man better, increasing your chances of predicting what he's going to do.
- It gives you more of an emotionally healthy relationship to fall back on if you encounter relationship problems—it's not a relationship that's based on sex.
- The sex could be better because you built up sexual tension.
- You never know when a man can throw out that you had sex too soon or accuse you of being promiscuous.
- It gives you more time to see if he is being honest about seeing you exclusively.
- If the relationship ends, you can never blame it on having sex too quickly.
- You'll feel more comfortable, and the sex will feel less awkward.

Trust Your Own Judgment

No matter how you play it, there are no formulas or guarantees about how things will turn out. There are women who have sex with men the first night they meet and they wind up marrying them. There are women who have sex with men right away and get dumped by them. Still other women wait months and months only to get hurt or rejected. Having sex with a man you're first getting to know is always a risk. But be a smart gambler, trust your own judgment, and try to accurately calculate the odds. And enjoy life; indulge yourself in pleasure, while still protecting yourself both emotionally and physically.

 ## The Men's Round Table Talks about Sex

In this section, the men will respond to a series of questions about sex.

 Do you expect a woman to have sex with you on the first date?

Bob

No. I don't expect much of anything from anyone other than mutual respect and common courtesy. People are far too unpredictable for me to expect anything these days.

Donald

No.

Doug

No, I don't. The first date usually is the Q+A—what makes you tick type of get-together. If there's chemistry, then things will progress and you develop fonder feelings toward each other and vice versa. For me, it depends on how well you communicate and relate to each other there—if it goes well, there maybe some sparks there.

Jerry

Sex on the first date is every man's dream, but I don't expect it. If or when it happens, I usually don't respect the woman as much as if she had waited. If I have sex with a woman on the first date, I feel it leaves almost no room for a future relationship outside of a sexual one and perhaps not even that since the thought of her being so easy makes me wonder how many other men she has been with.

Tom

I don't like the idea of having sex on a first date. It's too fast, too much physical intimacy before you establish any personal intimacy. It happened several times to me when I was separated from my first wife.

Many women I dated seemed desperate for a committed relationship and would do just about anything to get one. It was a poor strategy to try on me. I'm not a prude and did not lack for testosterone, yet some of those times, I couldn't perform. I think I was just plain scared. Once that happened, that was usually the end of the relationship right there. Some of the women, I guess, felt rejected by my performance problems; I felt somewhat embarrassed and inadequate. I remember reading a book at about that time by Herb Goldberg. I think it was called *The Male Mystique*. It had a chapter called "The Wisdom of the Penis." In it, Goldberg wrote something to the effect that men often are oblivious to their own feelings, but these feelings may nonetheless assert themselves in an inability to achieve or maintain an erection. The penis's failure at such times may well reflect hidden fears or doubts about starting a relationship with this particular woman or simply at this particular moment. There was certainly no medical reason to have a performance problem. Men, especially young men, have a tacit belief that they've got to "score" with as many women as possible. And, despite all our sophistication in sexual matters, we still feel guilty or ashamed or plain inadequate when we can't perform. Women, on the other hand, just say that they're not in the mood or that they're not attracted to the man "in that way," and they feel good about themselves.

Do you feel if a woman has sex with you too quickly (first time you meet, first date) that will affect your opinion of her?

Bob

It wouldn't necessarily affect my opinion of her positively or negatively. To me, it would be ridiculous to judge a potential relationship based on an initial sexual encounter. You need to get to know someone on a deeper level before you can start making judgments regarding the potential for a quality long-term relationship.

Donald

Yes. No matter how anyone spins this question, the honest answer is yes. Ladies—make us earn and work for that honor.

Doug

It really depends on the woman—if she is a sexually confident and straightforward type, then it's what she wants and it would be fine so long as we are feeling this mutually. There's a difference between this type of woman and a "loose" type that has no self-confidence and will sleep with anybody right away. Usually having a conversation with either of these types will let you know right away the character involved.

Jerry

Yes, it most certainly will.

Tom

It makes me think she is desperate.

 If a woman needs to date you for a while until she feels comfortable having sex with you, how would you feel?

Bob

It seems fair and reasonable, but it would also indicate to me that she might be uncomfortable about her sexuality and puts too much weight on notions regarding sex.

Donald

That is the point of question number four. Both parties are going to know when the time is right (obviously, men knowing sooner).

Doug

I don't mind that at all. As long as someone has the confidence about themselves and honesty to put that out there, that is totally fine with me. It's been my experience that on the second or third date things start to heat up and sex comes into play.

Jerry

Respect her for it, but everything has its limits.

Tom

That's OK. I prefer establishing a degree of personal intimacy before seeking physical intimacy. (I felt the same way even in my twenties. I was probably unusual in this regard, however.) This is not prudery on my part. It's just good practice. Not everybody is great in bed. Not everybody has a great body. Not every couple is in immediate agreement on how to do sex. You need to establish a personal bond first before you do the sex, so that if things aren't wonderful between the sheets, you have a solid relationship within which to try to work out compromises. And you have something of value in the relationship as a whole, so you can accept less than ideal in one part of it. Waiting until the relationship has a chance to develop is, I think, better strategy overall for women. If you have sex right away, when the two of you hardly know each other, all you are to him is a body, and you are competing with all the perfect bodies in his sexual fantasies. That's tough competition. It's better strategy to be a whole relationship first. His fantasy women can't compete with that. They don't laugh at his jokes or make him yummy treats or snuggle next to him in front of his favorite TV show. They don't listen sympathetically when he talks about a hard day at work or encourage him—without pushing or nagging—to try new things or even a new career.

Can you lose out on a man by holding off on sex until the relationship matures for a bit? Sure, but the men you lose that way are probably not marriage prospects to begin with: They demonstrate an unwillingness to respect differences and to compromise, and their fixation on immediate gratification suggests something about their maturity.

 If you're really crazy about a woman, how long is the longest you would wait until she feels ready to have sex with you?

Bob

Impossible to say. Every circumstance is different, but if I'm really into a woman, I want to do everything possible to make her feel comfortable. I guess the answer is: I'll wait as long as I have to, or until it's apparent to me that she's completely neurotic and it's time to bail out.

Donald

I am willing to wait for about three months. By that time, she and I should know if the relationship is worth continuing and whether or not we should take it to the next level.

Doug

Longest would be six to eight weeks, based on seeing someone at least once a week. Anything longer than that and I would start to wonder if there were some issues buried inside that she is reluctant to communicate.

Jerry

As long as it takes, but the problem there is how will I feel about her after getting something (sex) that I've been longing for for so long. Will that crazy feeling subside? My crazy feeling about her may diminish now after she gave it up. Never a good idea to wait too long.

Tom

Can't say. It depends on so many other factors. For one thing, if I think she's holding off because she is sex-averse in general, thinking of it as a distasteful chore a woman has to perform as a wifely obligation, I'll be gone in a flash. If, on the other hand, I think she really wants to be sure about the strength of our relationship before she is willing to let herself go, that's different.

I like sex as much as any man, but affection and love mean more to me. A woman who gives me a big smile and a warm good-night kiss will draw me to her much more than a woman who briskly takes me into her bedroom and whips off her clothes and says, in effect, "Do me."

 Does getting together just for sex (booty call) constitute a date in your mind?

Bob

I guess I could consider it a date. After all, it is two people getting together who are attracted to each other. I guess there are different degrees of dates.

Donald

NO. A booty call is just that, booty call.

Doug

It's the ultimate quickie date. If you really have sexual chemistry, then that's what works for the two of you—some people work amazingly well physically with each other and it's just a given that you don't need a fancy night out or special gift to get your libidos going.

Jerry

It could but when you're at the booty call stage I'd say you're past the dating stage.

Tom

Sure, why not?

 What makes you attracted to a woman?

Bob

Sensitivity, kindness, intelligence, inner strength, confidence, self-esteem, ambition, creativity, uniqueness, physical beauty. (I think I'm describing a goddess. I guess that's why I'm still single.)

Donald

Looks are important but not everything. Is she comfortable in her own skin? If she is—that is attractive.

Doug

When a woman is smart, funny, very confident/forward, and obviously physically appealing. For me, she must be sexy and exude self-confidence without being conceited. When a woman shows interest in you and is not afraid to put that out there, that is very sexy.

Jerry

Smart, funny, motivated, confident, independent (doesn't need me but makes me feel needed or wanted), physically attractive to me, of course, as well as sexually.

Tom

There are just so many things, it's difficult to list them all. Let me say, first, that a good face or figure will make me take a second look, but it doesn't hold my attention unless there's something else of interest. That might be a good sense of humor, an optimistic attitude, a good heart, somebody not totally superficial, i.e., she's interested in issues beyond herself and her immediate world. She's interested in understanding more than condemning or dismissing people out of hand. I guess what I'm getting to is that she's interesting and fun to talk to: it's not all about her and her circumstances. And, just as important, she's genuinely interested in learning about me.

 How would you advise women who are dating when to have sex with a man so that he doesn't think that she is promiscuous, and she doesn't risk getting rejected because he thinks she's too frustrating?

Bob

Be concerned with what makes you comfortable. You are not a mind reader, and even if you were, why would you want to do anything you aren't comfortable with doing simply to appease someone you don't even know that well? Be yourself and don't worry about rejection. If someone rejects you for being yourself, why would you want to pursue a person who doesn't want to be with you?

Donald

Ladies, ultimately, you have to make this call. Hopefully, by looking at the answers to the above questions, you will know when the time is right. You need to know that this is a guy who you like to be around, who makes you feel good, who respects you and is available for you too.

Doug

My advice is to just talk about it. If you feel attracted to someone just let them know—things will progress from there. I think books like *The Rules* have really damaged women's and men's confidence in each other. People are waiting for the other person to act a certain way or say some-thing—it's just not normal that you should be looking for someone who seems normal from the start. If you have to play all these games and act a certain way to get them to respond, then you yourself are not being real. It all boils down to learning to communicate and relate, especially what you want from someone and/or a relationship.

Jerry

The best thing I can say is wait at least a week from the first time you went out with him. Of course, that would imply that you spent a lot of time on the phone with him at least or saw him at least a few times that week. Don't think you want to wait more than three months . . . in fact that might be too long. But the best advice, I think, would be go with your feeling, that's all. And if he reacts the wrong way about your decision, then he is not the right one for you after all.

Tom

No simple rules apply here because men are not all the same. You have to know the man and be able to judge accurately how he feels about you. If you and he are really enjoying each other's company and he is affectionate but doesn't push for sex, let him decide.

If he's a great date but pushes for sex from date one, you might give in after a few dates, holding him off until then by letting him know how happy you are with him and how rapidly your defenses are crumbling date by date. Most guys won't give up if they think they are making some progress.

Chapter 11

Dating Etiquette

- Are you and a girlfriend interested in the same guy?
- Wondering when to confess a sticky secret about yourself to a new man?
- Unsure how to extricate yourself from a blind date with a man you're not interested in?
- Debating if you should offer to chip in on a first date?

If you answered yes to even one of these questions, you will greatly benefit from this chapter on etiquette. In actuality, every aspect of the dating experience—from first meeting (should you drop hints you're interested or simply ask him out?) to determining the best way to break off the relationship—is fraught with sensitive and sometimes bizarre potential scenarios that demand a deft touch.

When in doubt about how to react to a particular situation, remember the Golden Rule of Etiquette: treat others with respect, kindness and diplomacy, and—very important—expect the same treatment in return. New York–based life coach Beth Schoenfeldt puts it this way, "The barometer of how to behave is to ask yourself how you would act toward a really good friend."

Is lying to spare someone's feelings ever the best choice? Schoenfeldt says, "The kind thing in modern etiquette is to tell the truth as diplomatically as possible. It may hurt for the moment, but it's always best to get things out in the open."

Now that we have the big picture, let's fill in the particulars.

At First Sight

Stephanie, an attractive twenty-eight-year-old computer programmer, came to see me because she was bothered by her shyness around men. She blamed her passiveness for ruining her chances with Ken. When she first spotted Ken at a party, she felt immensely drawn to him. He seemed to notice her as well and came over to start a conversation. Unfortunately, Stephanie was at the party with her close friend Carly, who quickly monopolized the conversation among the three singles.

"I felt so frustrated," Stephanie explained. "I tried to subtly signal Carly to lay off, that I really liked this guy! But she's very competitive—she always needs every man to fall under her spell."

Carly didn't take the hint and Stephanie, uncomfortable at the notion of competition, became very quiet. Soon Ken and Carly were flirting and making weekend plans.

Did Stephanie have a right to be angry at Carly? Had Carly taken advantage of Stephanie's passive nature?

The Harsh Truth

All is fair in love and war.

The women essentially met Ken at the same point in time. Stephanie had no prior claim and made no serious attempt to persuade Carly to socialize elsewhere. Even if she had, Carly had no obligation to just walk away.

Yes, the friendship here should be paramount. However, both women have an obligation to be considerate of one another. Say Stephanie had briefly dated Ken and *then* he'd asked out her friend. Carly would have had a clear obligation, not to ask Stephanie's permission, but to inform her of the date. Stephanie likely wouldn't have felt pleased, but at least everything would have been aboveboard. If Carly truly liked Ken but *didn't* go on the date to spare her friend's feelings, Carly would have become resentful.

It would have been entirely appropriate for Stephanie to insert herself into the conversation in a gentle way. In order to take advantage of potential dating situations, Barbara had to learn to step up her confidence level.

Janet, a thirty-three-year-old real-estate executive, learned the hard way that handling situations with subterfuge inevitably backfires. She was at Barnes & Noble thumbing through the latest fiction best-sellers when a "plump, sweating man in a magenta suit" tried to pick her up with the memorable line, "So, you like to read?" Janet had no interest in pursuing a conversation but wanted to end the pickup attempt in as inoffensive a way as possible. She said she'd love to stay and chat but had an appointment across town in twenty minutes. Mr. Magenta looked disappointed but obligingly let Janet slip past him.

However, she didn't leave the store—she often cruised for dates in bookstores. A few minutes later, Janet met a man she was very attracted to in the self-help section. Janet's enjoyment of their conversation was considerably spoiled when she looked up and saw Mr. Magenta looking at her with a very hostile expression.

What is the best way to discourage unwanted advances from a stranger? Here are a few variations on the honesty with diplomacy tactic:

- The direct, stern approach: "Thank you (pause), but I don't think so. And I wish you well on your search."
- The polite but firm approach: "I'm really flattered and you seem like a nice person, but I don't see us as a match"; "I've enjoyed talking to you but I've got to say goodbye now."
- If he is persistent: "I've tried to say I'm not interested in a nice way, but you're not getting the message. I'm not interested and it's time for you to move away."

Many men have told me that they are afraid to approach an appealing woman because they've been rudely rejected on so many occasions. Imagine yourself in their shoes and you'll know how hard it is to put your ego on the line and walk up to a good-looking guy you'd love to date. Remember, treat others as you would like to be treated.

Some examples of how *not* to respond to polite but unwanted pickup attempts:

- I'm truly insulted. How dare you think someone like me would be interested in someone like you?
- You wouldn't be so bad if you did something about your weight and that lame outfit.
- Sure, here's my number. I'm looking forward to your call (after you've changed one of the digits in your telephone number to ensure he never reaches you).

Women as Initiators

It's commonly believed that men traditionally make the first move. However, according to a 2004 survey conducted by Grand Marnier on Conversations That Matter, women more frequently start the ball rolling than men. The survey results confirm that times have changed—dating etiquette says it's perfectly acceptable for women to go after what (whom!) they want. Indeed many men welcome being the pursued versus being the pursuer. However, you don't want to appear too forward. So what's the best approach?

According to Don Gabor, communications trainer and author of *Words That Win: What to Say to Get What You Want* (Prentice Hall Press, 2003), women who successfully make the initial contact do so in a variety of ways—it can be via body signals (eye contact, smile) and/or an opening line. However, he cautions, "Don't bring up controversial topics like politics or religion. The best conversation starters are simple ones—for example, you say to the person sitting next to you on the park bench, "Hi, I'm Sue. How has your day been so far?"

Other openers:

- The complimentary approach: What a nice sweater!
- The inquisitive approach: Is that camera hard to operate? I've always wanted to learn to take a good photo.
- Is that a good book? It's been on my list for months.

Moving Things Along

Gabor says, "The most important rule in dating etiquette is knowing how to listen." Once you've initiated the conversation, be sure not to monopolize it.

So you've started a conversation and things are going well—he laughs at your jokes; you laugh at his. How do you bring it to the next level? Sarah, a thirty-eight-year-old Brooklyn hairstylist and former client, has had success sealing the deal. "If I meet someone and he asks for my number, great. Otherwise, I suggest it. You've got to go for what you want in life. I'll say something like, 'So, you've been wanting to see that movie too? Perhaps the two of us can go together one evening?' or 'Maybe we can hang out sometime.'" Sarah adds, "Often he's just shy so his reaction to my being forward is relief that I've done the hard part."

Online Dating

Online dating has evolved into a legitimate, even respected method for singles to find each other. But the impersonality of this medium can lend itself to ruptures in etiquette. After all, these men are total strangers. Your first priority is caution, not politeness. These men are total strangers, and no one will fault your manners if you are cautious.

So here are some rules to follow to make your online experience a safe and productive one.

May I Have This Cyber Dance?

As in real life, men often make the first move in the world of cyber dating. But if you find someone who really appeals to you, there's no harm in your making the first contact. It will likely be the highlight of his day. Just like in real life, the best opening is one in which you mention something complimentary or thoughtful about his profile. If you notice he's an avid swimmer and you are too, now is the time to bring it up. However, this isn't time for any true confessions! Refrain from sending lengthy narratives about your agonizing divorce or terrifying phobias. If you "click," there'll be plenty of time for that later.

What about men who are totally unappealing? A short, polite e-mail will suffice: "Thank you so much for your note. You seem like a great guy, but I don't see us as a match. I wish you luck in your search."

Naturally, when shopping you really want to see the goods before purchasing. But what if he doesn't post a photo? Sandy, a thirty-three-year-old journalist, met her fiancé online. She contacted him even though his profile didn't include a picture. "I didn't mention his lack of pictures in my first e-mail to him. Since he'd already seen my photo when it became obvious the interest was mutual, I asked if he had one he could send to me, although I stressed it wasn't essential as long as he was able to give me an accurate description."

Unfortunately inaccuracies—oh, let's call them lies!—are common in the online dating world. Routinely people lie about their age, height, and weight, and decade-old photos. You should be honest, and in your profile state that more than a buff body or a full head of hair in a man, you value honesty.

Other online faux pas:

- PROFILES OR E-MAILS THAT ARE ALL CAPS. This is considered shouting in cyberland.
- Sending a cookie-cutter response to every man. He'll assume it's your standard greeting to prospective dates.
- Being an "emoticon" offender. Don't be too casual in e-mails. Avoid overusing smiley faces or "lol" (lots of laughs).
- Hesitating to push for a real-world meeting. If he seems content to maintain an online relationship (he keeps writing, "We must get together *sometime*"), don't hesitate after a few reciprocal meetings to suggest politely he set a date. You don't need a pen pal.
- Not insisting you meet in a public place. It isn't rude to insist on ground rules to protect yourself.
- Investing a lot of time in the "meet." This also applies to online dating. If you take the relationship into the real world, start simple—meet for a cup of coffee and a muffin or glass of wine.

It's not only inexpensive but after forty-five minutes or so you may politely take your leave.

Sight No Longer Unseen

If you like him and don't hear from him for a few days after seeing him, you can shoot off a quick e-mail: "Thanks so much for the drink and the company. Hope you're doing well." If you hear from him, great. If not, do not e-mail him again. Instead, get back to the dating site. Remember, it's a numbers game.

If after the meeting you decide he's just not right for you, don't do anything, and pray he doesn't contact you. If you do hear from him, you can respond with an e-mail along the lines of, "While it was fun meeting you, I just didn't feel we were compatible enough to pursue a relationship. But I wish you all the best."

There is no need to be embarrassed or coy about cyberdating. In the end it doesn't matter how you met, just that you met.

First Dates

Once you've initiated contact and have decided you like each other it's time to meet. First dates are inevitably tension-filled, awkward affairs for understandable reasons. Thus few would disagree with this definition of a first date: a necessary evil. Like job interviews, you have to get through them in order to get to the goal—in this case, a shot at a relationship. You're nervous, frightened, and *rightly* determined to put your best foot forward. It's easy in such a stressful situation to say and/or do things that will make the other person want to yell "sorry" over his shoulder as he runs for the hills at the end of the evening.

How can you make a good first impression and build a foundation for what could be the start of something beautiful?

Take this pop quiz.

On a first date, acceptable topics to discuss include:

A. Your abortion
B. Your hatred of men
C. Your aversion to eating meat
D. Your desire to know his salary

Choices a, b, and d are red-flag topics—either it's information he doesn't need to know yet, will never want to know, or that will make him think you're a gold digger.

A first date is the time to be yourself—at your most sparkling and self-confident. Trot out your most entertaining tales, like your summer trip to Budapest or how your knowledge of first aid saved a restaurant patron who had collapsed midmeal. As I mentioned in the online dating section, when you're trying to make a good impression you should resist the urge to tell your intensely traumatic stories. For example, here are some subjects you should not discuss on the first date:

- What antidepressants you're on
- Your chronic physical ailments
- Your most traumatic breakup

And here are topics that are wonderful first-date fodder:

- The winter you spent as an exchange student in Italy
- Your favorite hobby
- Your passion for your career

In other words, it's fine to discuss things that are or were exciting parts of your life. It's also fine to ask him questions to get to know him better. It's appropriate to ask him what he does for a living, where he lives, what his interests are, what his marital or relationship status is, if he has children and if they live with him. You don't want to sound like a DA, but at the same time, it's self-protective to know who and what you are dealing with. You could be dealing with another Scott Peterson—and you don't want to be the next Amber Frey. Besides, he'll probably enjoy your rapt attention and interest in him.

Who Pays?

Perhaps the most awkward first-date dilemma is determining if you should offer to pay your share.

Amy, a successful thirty-year-old mortgage broker, recalls the moment she knew Warren, a forty-year-old pediatrician, wasn't for her. Amy recalls, "We'd known each other socially for months and I'd been so excited when he finally asked me on a date. I suggested a moderately priced Thai restaurant, but he insisted on taking me to an expensive new seafood place. I was prepared to order the least expensive items, but after he went for lobster, so did I. He said, 'Good, I like to see a woman enjoy herself.'"

When the check came Amy was totally shocked as Warren looked it over and said, "Your share is $65.50, but it's OK if you just give me $40." Amy handed over the money and felt she'd gotten away cheap. "Imagine if I'd gotten emotionally connected before discovering his true nature!"

Yes, Warren should have paid for dinner, especially since he issued the invitation and encouraged Amy to eat to her heart's content. But is it always the man's responsibility to pay and pay and pay?

Jill came to see me when her fiancé threatened to break off the engagement. The twenty-five-year-old wedding planner revealed a major reason for her troubles when she told me that she'd never paid for one meal or play or vacation during the couple's two years together. "A man should pay during the entire courtship until the marriage," she told me, adding, "It should be his privilege to treat his lady. In return, it's her place to be loving and nurturing."

This attitude is not only retro, it's dangerous as well. If you abdicate sole monetary responsibility to a man, not only are you putting an inordinate amount of financial pressure on him (unless he's Donald Trump), you are giving him all the power. Once you're married, he may feel justified in making all decisions, from where to dine to what car to buy, and pretty soon you may come to realize that you're not always happy with *his* decisions.

While these days many women insist on paying their share, it's still commonly expected that the man initially forks it over. Betsy, a thirty-two-year-old teacher, says, "A man who pays on the first date is a class act. A man who expects you to dig into your wallet is cheap. You can't assume he's going to pay, so you should offer. If he accepts, that's a bad sign. I believe all things should be equal, but I also believe that a man who doesn't pick up the check on the first date is probably an emotionally stingy individual." She adds, "Down the road the financial dynamics between the couple will change. It's unrealistic to expect the guy to continue picking up every check."

Where there are no hard-and-fast etiquette rules when it comes to dating and money, you can't go wrong if you adhere to the following guidelines:

- On a first date, choose a reasonably priced restaurant and don't order the most expensive items on the menu.
- Expect the man to pay for the first date but offer to contribute.
- When he pays, say thank you.
- If you have no romantic interest in him, *insist* on paying your share (many men feel burned by women who have soaked them for an expensive meal, then won't take their call).
- If he acts like treating you to an expensive dinner entitles him to dessert at your place, set him straight. Sexual favors are not on the menu.
- If he earns much more than you and pays for most dates, make an effort to even the scales by buying him little presents, making home-cooked meals, or buying dessert after the movie.
- If you earn much more, it's fine for you to grab most of the checks. But hopefully he's doing those small things, like bringing you flowers and giving you massages.
- If your boyfriend is going through a financial hardship, make more of an effort to pay on dates. However, don't lend him money. Loans and love don't mix.

Post–First Date

Everyone experiences a lot of anxiety in the beginning of a relationship, and with good reason. You're putting yourself out there and there's a chance you might get hurt. So if a first date is tough, the period immediately after it can be harder to endure than listening to fingernails on a chalkboard. Here's what happened to my client Leslie.

The twenty-nine-year-old magazine editor had a great first date. Sparks flew and every other sentence out of Kevin's mouth was, "I'd love to take you to hear my favorite band . . ." and "You'll flip when you try this fantastic Korean place I discovered tucked away on an obscure side street . . ."

The kiss goodbye was passionate and Leslie was positive she'd hear from Kevin the next day, especially since he'd borrowed her umbrella, clutching it to his heart and proclaiming, "Gee, now I know you'll see me again."

Imagine her shock when he didn't get in touch. Three days later she was climbing the walls but hesitant to call him. "I believe the guy should contact the woman. Period. If he doesn't, it's not because he's had a car crash or a family emergency. It's because he's not interested. But this case was a bit extreme. He'd acted so gung ho about me."

Maybe *too* gung ho. Men who do everything but propose on the first date typically love romance and are born aggressors—they love the thrill of the chase. However, when something has the potential of being real, they can become scared and pull away. These men often don't realize the emotional damage they inflict on women.

The best response to silence is usually a matching silence. Why give him the satisfaction of knowing he's "gotten" you? However, Leslie had been misled into giving away property (not a $4 street umbrella but a $40 Nicole Miller). Four days after their date, she left a message on his cell phone asking for the umbrella. No answer. There was still no point in getting vindictive. Rudeness in response to rudeness can net hostility. Kevin and Leslie had met through Kim, a mutual friend who also worked in Kevin's office. Leslie e-mailed Kevin at work and simply requested him to bring the umbrella in to work and hand it over to Kim, who knew the whole situation. Kevin did as asked.

Leslie said afterward, "I was dying to explode at him. He'd been horrible to me. But he clearly didn't have a conscience I could prick. Insulting him wouldn't get what I wanted. So I acted businesslike and my property was returned."

Kathy, a thirty-three-year-old dental technician, had the opposite problem. She'd had a "blah" first date, at evening's end shaking his hand and saying, "Nice to meet you. All the best." No mixed signals—a clear brush-off. Only Tom didn't know he was history. He kept calling and e-mailing. Kathy, who can't bear to be unkind, avoided his calls. This was unintentionally cruel. Although she wasn't encouraging him, he was looking at her lack of response as a positive sign . . . or at least not a negative one.

I advised her to call and nicely but definitely affirm that while he was a nice person, she didn't see a future for them. She did this and Tom stopped bothering her.

Discovering He's Mr. Not So Perfect

Your new boyfriend is a great guy. He's sweet, considerate, fun, sexy, and definitely into you. But alas, he does have a few quirks or small flaws that in time might start to grate. The dilemma for you is figuring out how to tell him what bothers you without hurting his feelings . . . much. After all, he is overall a keeper.

A common dilemma early in a relationship is figuring out exactly when you can commence smoothing out your new boyfriend's rough edges. Say he has a terrible sense of style or talks with his mouth full? You want to correct what you perceive as his "flaws" but are afraid if you say anything before the *l* word much less *c* word has been spoken, he'll think you're a shrew and bolt?

First, ask yourself if your dissatisfaction with this aspect of him is justified or simply a manifestation of your commitment phobia, meaning your pattern is a man gets close and you find reasons to push him away. Especially if you're Ms. Ambivalent Woman!

OK, what if you're not afraid of intimacy? You just want to "help" him be the best man he can be. Remember how I mentioned at the beginning of the chapter to be honest yet diplomatic? This is an instance when the latter part of that directive is especially important.

Try to hold out until the relationship is at least a month old. Now consider this: the most polite way to criticize someone is to do it in the guise of a compliment. Tell him how much you admire him—he's sexy, smart, kind, considerate—but there is one small thing that's been bothering you. It's not a big deal, but you wonder if he's aware that sometimes he talks with his mouth full? You only bring it up because an ex once told you that you had an annoying habit of banging your spoon against your cup loudly and continuously. (It's good to admit to your own flaw.) You'd never been aware of this habit so have been working to correct it. Assure him his habit is not a big deal, you just thought he might want to know he has it.

If he's hurt or angry, let it go—at least until you're more solid as a couple. Pick your battles. If he wants to change, help him but always, always be sensitive and caring.

Saying Goodbye Gracefully

When you're dating, there will be times that you're just not attracted to a man. But how can you say goodbye with decency and sensitivity? Well, different situations call for different measures. These tips will help you say goodbye gracefully in any situation.

Boring Blind Dates

Not every date is going to be love at first sight. So if you ever find yourself in the middle of an excruciatingly boring blind date, don't bolt at first sight. And don't let him see that you're bored. Be friendly. Hang in for forty-five minutes or so (remember, blind dates should be quick dates); then say you've got to get going, but it was nice meeting him. Or a simple, "Bye now. Have a great day." The key is to project friendliness without encouragement. For instance, say something like, "It was nice meeting you. I wish you luck at finding what you're looking for."

After You've Exchanged Saliva

After a blind date, or even just a few casual dates, breaking up is a relatively simple matter. It can probably be done in a phone call. But once you've become a quasi couple and/or been naked under the sheets, it's not kind to let your answering machine do the breaking up for you. If he keeps calling, tell him you really enjoy being with him, but:

A. You're looking for different things in a relationship. Therefore it's best to make a clean break. For example, say, "I want to have kids at some point and you definitely don't want children. That's a major incompatibility, so I feel strongly that we should end things now." Or as I mentioned previously, "You are a nice person but I just don't see a future for us."

B. You can always use the standard, "I'm just not ready for a relationship right now" or "I'm completely focusing on my career right now."

C. There's always the old "I've gone back to my ex-boyfriend" excuse. This way he doesn't feel insulted or hurt.

After Several Months and/or Using Each Other's Toothbrush

Breaking up becomes more involved than a quick, "Sorry, it's over." He's got feelings and you need to respect them. A client of mine found that out the hard way. When twenty-six-year-old Rebecca initially tried to end her four-month relationship with Frank, she did it at the end of a date with a quick, "You're a great guy but I think we're on different tracks." Her hope was he'd go home to nurse his wounds, but he begged to come in and talk. Three pots of coffee later he was finally on his way and Rebecca was drained but happy. "He was still sad but he understood where I was coming from and that I wasn't going to change my mind. We've actually become friends and double-dated with our current partners."

Like Rebecca, you owe your about-to-be ex some face-to-face time and the opportunity to ask all the questions he needs to achieve closure. Again, answer honestly but not hurtfully. It's not necessary to negate the whole relationship when you leave. It is kind to validate what you once had as you're acknowledging that it's time to move on. Rebecca ended things with Frank because spending time with him was a big yawn. Instead of saying he was boring, she told him that ultimately she felt they wouldn't have enough things in common to make it. He was *Crossfire*; she was *Fear Factor.*

In general, how much you owe a man an explanation depends on the duration and intensity of your relationship. In all cases be decisive. If you hem and haw he'll think there's hope, so don't act ambivalent. Be direct but not sadistic. Don't transfer anger toward your ex-boyfriend who "done you wrong" onto a man who cares for you but just can't reciprocate those feelings. However, you don't have to be a victim either. If he gets angry at you, then he needs to work through these feelings on his own. Leave him feeling that you enjoyed spending time with him. But leave. If you're done don't let him talk you into giving him one more chance. You owe him kindness, not your head on a platter.

Chapter 12

The Art of Playing It Cool

Sometimes men start to distance or show a lack of enthusiasm after they've gone out with you a few times. Often it's not because of their waning interest in you, but rather their fears of engulfment or their struggle with intimacy issues. Obviously, this can make a woman feel very insecure despite her insight into his behavior. No matter what, it is in your best interest to play it cool despite how anxious he makes you feel. How do you pull this off? By regulating your "internal state" when you think you're going into panic mode. Here's how it's done the next time your new guy:

- Doesn't want to see you as often as you'd like
- Doesn't respond to your phone message, e-mail, or text message as soon as you'd like
- Cancels your next date
- Doesn't call when he says he will
- Doesn't call more than three days after a date
- Doesn't call as much as you'd like
- Does anything to indicate that he is losing interest in you

Do not freak out or "cling" to him! No calling him, no going over to his house, no e-mailing him, no instant messaging him, no text messaging him. Instead, put all of your energy and focus on "regulating your internal state." In nonclinical terms, you need to calm yourself down! Chill!

OK, here's the science behind it: When you go into panic mode when a guy doesn't call, your mind goes into high alert, adrenaline soars through your body, and the frontal lobe of your brain, which controls your logical thinking, shuts down as your limbic system takes over, which is what causes you to act clingy.

So, when the man you are dating or want to date causes this bio-chemical mess, you need to fight back by doing whatever it takes not to act out your anxiety, panic, fear of loss, or abandonment. This is the art of regulating your internal state, which can be very challenging indeed. This doesn't mean to not be in touch with your emotions and stop express-ing them. You can express your feelings all you want, just not to him. Let-ting all of your emotions out on the man who is triggering them doesn't accomplish anything. In fact, it often scares men away, even good men who are psychologically equipped for a healthy relationship. So, it's essen-tial to do whatever it takes to do nothing. Instead turn your energy and attention to what you can do to make yourself feel better. The operant words here are distract, refocus, and self-nurture.

The next time you have the urge to leave him a voice mail (the fifth one in two hours), consider the following techniques:

- Take a bath or shower
- Watch a video or DVD that you find entertaining and distracting
- Get out of the house
- Get a manicure or pedicure
- Visit a friend
- Exercise
- Put on a meditation or relaxation tape
- Go shopping
- Go to a movie
- Have a facial or message
- Cook
- Go to an art gallery
- Plan a trip
- Go to a museum
- Get out of town
- Eat chocolates or your favorite dessert
- Do yoga
- Call for an emergency therapy session

- Read a book
- Call someone in your support system
- Go to the beach
- Go to dinner with friends
- Do something athletic
- Call all of your friends in your phone book
- Attend any parties

On a sheet of paper, make a list of five comfort activities that soothe you. Keep the paper somewhere that you can see it, such as on your refrigerator, and refer to it when you need it.

Another suggestion is trying to relax your body to help combat the adrenaline overload. You can start out by doing a body scan to check out how tense you are. Filling out the following writing exercises will help guide you. You can set the mood by lighting a scented candle or putting on some soothing music.

BODY SCAN WRITING EXERCISES

Stomach

- Does it hurt?
- Do you feel nauseated?

Your Head

- Do you have a headache?
- Do you feel dizzy?

Your Back

- Does it hurt?
- Do you feel tense?

Your Shoulders

- Do they hurt?
- Do they feel tense?

Your Neck

- Does it hurt?
- Does it feel strained?

Your Legs

- Do they hurt?
- Are your muscles tense?

BODY SCAN WRITING EXERCISES

Emotions Checklist

Now it's time to check out what's going on with your feelings. Burn another candle and continue the writing exercises. You're healing yourself by focusing all of your attention on "YOU" rather than being so preoccupied with "HIM."

DO YOU FEEL?

Hungry
Dizzy
Nauseated
Elated
Paranoid
Angry
Enraged
Numb
Depressed
Sad
Happy
Relieved
In despair

Reward Time

After doing this hard emotional work, reward yourself. Try some of the suggestions from the list at the beginning of this chapter. My choice would be chocolate ice cream. Maybe a massage or a facial could do the trick for you. The point is to nurture yourself!

"Going Deeper"

Some women have more difficulty acting cool because any type of abandonment by a man stirs up lots of deep feelings in them as a result of trauma they might have incurred earlier in their lives. Unfortunately, the more traumas a woman has endured, the more work she has to do not to be so drastically affected by a man's behavior. In other words, a woman who has had minimal trauma in her life might just roll a man's disappointing behavior right off her shoulder. So to not get so bent out of shape over men and not personalize their behavior so much, it is necessary to develop insight into yourself. Self-knowledge is a tremendously powerful resource and tool. However, in order to develop this insight, you must be consciously aware of trauma that occurred in your life. Jot down your reactions to the traumatic situations you may have experienced, as you read through the list.

TRAUMA THAT CAN OCCUR IN CHILDHOOD
- Sexually abused
- Emotionally abused
- Physically abused
- Verbally abused
- Your parents divorced
- One of your parents died
- You were bullied, made fun of, or harassed in school
- You were too ill to go to school
- Your sibling died
- You were living in poverty

TRAUMA THAT OCCURRED IN ADULTHOOD
- Breakups with men
- Emotional or physically abusive relationships with men
- Rape
- Physical violence/mugging/attacked
- Losing a job

- An abusive boss
- Coping with chronic illness
- Losing a child
- Losing a parent you were attached to
- Losing a spouse

Be aware that trauma is retroactive, so this means that when a new trauma occurs, all of your past traumas get triggered. So if he doesn't return your call, breaks up with you, or hurts you in any way, it could be activating old wounds. You can immediately help yourself by remembering that you're not a helpless child anymore. You are a grown woman now, with myriad resources. This situation with the guy doesn't have to turn into a big melodrama if you don't let it. You have the power to change your life around now. You do not have to repeat history.

When you're not in crisis mode or in a state of panic, try to resolve your trauma so that you're less affected by your past. You can also use this time to develop more coping skills. How do you do this?

- Psychotherapy
- Group therapy
- Energy therapies (EMDR, reiki, etc.)
- Meditation
- Workshops
- Twelve-step programs

Despite hard work, you may still experience that panic occasionally if a man upsets you, but it will be more manageable. You'll be better able to control your emotions and behavior rather than feeling victimized by your past negative experiences. Wanting to cling will merely be a feeling you can work with rather than a part of your emotional repertoire.

Chapter 13

The Three Month Mark— To Stay or Not to Stay, That Is the Question

Moving On from a New Relationship That's Not Working

If you are at the three-month mark, and totally happy with the man you're dating, skip this chapter. However, if you are concerned about whether you should continue dating, then read on.

First, how do you tell that the two of you are not turning into a couple—at least the kind of couple that you have in mind? To begin with, there are some signs and hints that you might get from him that would indicate that maybe he's not really available to be a member of your "couplehood." You already know most of these:

1. He doesn't want to see you on holidays.
2. He hasn't introduced you to his parents or other close relatives.
3. When he's with you, he frequently discusses other women he knows or dates.
4. He doesn't include you in his vacation plans.
5. He doesn't introduce you as his girlfriend or refer to himself as your boyfriend.
6. If he sees you on weekends, he gets annoyed if you call him during the week.
7. While you're sharing about an issue that's obviously very important to you, you can tell that he's not really listening or interested.
8. The two of you haven't had sex yet, and it's not because you're pushing him away.
9. You see him only at his initiative, and you can never be sure when he will call or want to see you.
10. You're still not dating on Saturday night.
11. When you call him, he doesn't call you back for days.
12. He hasn't introduced you to his friends or coworkers.

Now, there also could be signs you're getting within yourself—your reactions to him and his behavior—that indicate "it's not working for you."

1. You never think about him when he's not around.
2. You have no sexual chemistry for him no matter how much time you give it.
3. There are aspects of his personal grooming that you can't stand: his dirty fingernails, his sloppy attire, uncombed hair, bad breath, or body odor.
4. His financial management practices conflict dramatically with yours—maybe he spends recklessly or maybe he hates to part with money.
5. He is addicted to something—maybe gambling, drugs, alcohol, or weird sex.
6. He doesn't take care of his health—for example, he's overweight and eats nonstop, or he never sees a dentist or doctor.
7. He is narcissistic. He talks continuously about himself and never listens to you. Everything is all about him, him, him, with no room for you.
8. He's too far-out, "weird," or unconventional for you.
9. He is excessively critical and judgmental—you can never come up to his standards on anything.
10. He is emotionally abusive: he teases you about your weight or looks, tells you you're stupid, or compares you unfavorably to other women. He frequently makes you cry.
11. His values are different from yours. He believes in taking advantage of people, or he is a bigot.
12. His life goals are different. He expresses no interest in settling down. Instead, he talks constantly of good times he plans for himself as a single man.

So, if you are unsure if the relationship is working, what is the next step?

Step One: Explore Possibilities

Him Changing

Maybe you can get him to change, even a little bit, for the sake of the relationship. You can try talking to him about what's bothering you and see whether he is willing to at least consider the possibility of changing. It could be that he's not really aware of the problem and that it affects other relationships he has, as well. Recognition might dawn if you tell him that he doesn't really pay attention when you talk and that affects how you feel about him. Of course, if that's his problem, he has undoubtedly heard that from other women. He may want to continue to chalk that up to "women." But he may now be ready to get serious about it. You might mean more to him than he lets you know.

Maybe there's something to be negotiated: he, in turn, might be having a problem with some aspect of your behavior. If he doesn't seem to accept you as his girlfriend, maybe there's a problem that he sees in you that prevents him from doing this. Do you have some of the traits of Ms. Alienator or Ms. Controlling that are turning him off? It's important to see if he has the emotional capacity to grapple with relationship problems instead of running away.

WARNING

There is the possibility that by talking to him, he could hurt your feelings. He might tell you he doesn't see you on Saturday nights because he is just not falling in love with you. The truth shall set us free, but it can hurt like hell; so if you are overly sensitive, you might also consider ending things and walking away without the talk. But then again, you'll never know what would have happened if you had tried.

You Changing

Or maybe—and this is much harder—you can try to be as objective as you can about what it is about you that he finds unsatisfactory. Maybe he's experiencing you as excessively demanding. Or maybe you accuse him of being "judgmental" or "critical" when he's only presenting an alternative point of view or pointing out objectively where your facts or logic are wrong. You might review other failed relationships you've had. What was the problem? Maybe there's a pattern that you can detect, a problem within you that you can start working on. Are you Ms. Ambivalent? Are you devaluing him? Are you being way too picky? Are your own commitment issues being stirred up from the relationship with him? Ask people in your support system for their objective opinions.

* WARNING *

Don't use any of the self-exploration suggestions I've mentioned as an excuse to berate yourself and take all the blame. Sometimes women think they are the problem because they want to have control of the situation. Maybe he's just not the one for you. As ol' Siggy Freud said, "Sometimes a cigar is just a cigar."

Step Two: Give It Some Time

Don't jump into making conclusions. See if exploring and discussing leads to positive changes. Be encouraged with even small changes for the better. Even if the problem is entirely his, be openly appreciative of progress he makes, as long as he seems sincere about wanting to do the work.

Use this time to re-examine your feelings about not wanting to be with him. Be 100 percent certain you're not making decisions based on your own relationship issues you need to work on and resolve.

Step Three: It's Just Not Working

You tried exploring and negotiating, and you made sure that you were not overlooking something very important to you. He still shows up for dates drunk, or he keeps putting you down. Despite his promises to change, nothing has changed. You've re-examined your own feelings over and over, and you just can't see doing the long haul with him. You're afraid you'll be "settling" and live to regret it.

Now is when you have to liquidate a bad investment. Forget about all the time you've spent on this relationship. In accounting terms, that's called "sunk costs," which means it's lost, gone forever, and you can't get it back no matter what you do. What you must do now is swiftly and as painlessly as possible, cut off further investment of your most valuable asset—your time—and seek a new person to invest in, or stay on your own.

Step Four: Don't Go Back

Once you've ended the relationship with him, don't go back! This is where so many women mess up. He's out of their life. They're lonely. They begin to think of reasons why they can restart the relationship while still retaining a shred of self-respect. I once heard Tony Robbins say that in his research he discovered the one thing all great leaders had in common was never to second-guess a decision they made. You can be great, too!

Chapter 14

How to Create Romantic Opportunities

There are just not enough great guys out there to take care of all the women who want one, so you can't afford to pass up any missed opportunities. Therefore, I'm going to tell you how to transform a casual, everyday situation into a romantic one.

If you are going to succeed in your dating journey, you may have to be more aggressive in meeting new men . . . even more aggressive than is comfortable for you. Look at it positively: Women can now be fully equal to men in every area that counts. If men can aggressively pursue women, why can't women aggressively pursue new men who pique their interest? Actually, as you know, many women already do and have been quite successful at it. So let's put aside our inhibitions and go after what (or rather, whom) we want. I will be covering two general situations in this chapter:

1. You see a man (or men) on a regular basis, but in a routine situation, such as a job.
2. You see a man (or men) in a one-time situation, such as a lecture or a professional office.

The Regular-Basis Situation

There he is, just like he is every workday, sitting at his desk on the telephone or at the computer. You like him, you think he's unattached, you think he likes you, but nothing is happening. Where do you go from here? Back to risk/reward analysis. Here are some signs that suggest he would be receptive, therefore a low risk:

SIGNS HE'S RECEPTIVE

- You notice him looking at you when he doesn't see that you notice
- He likes to talk to you about things outside work, especially his personal life
- He wants to know about your personal life
- He does favors for you, sometimes without your even asking him—for example, he takes your coffee cup with him when he goes to refill his own
- He gazes at your body
- He gazes into your eyes
- He flirts with you
- Your instincts tell you he is interested in you
- The two of you have a strong common interest outside work, such as politics, movies, or books, which you spend a lot of time talking about—workplace griping (agreeing that your boss is an idiot or that a certain coworker is always sucking up) doesn't count

High-Risk Situations

When is it too much of a risk, even when one or more of the signs are present?

- You work closely together (in close physical proximity) and you can't afford to leave the job
- You're both working on a project that is very important to you
- He is your supervisor or boss
- You're his boss or supervisor
- He's your best friend, and you can't take even a sliver of a chance of losing him

If you make a play and get rejected, you may risk being reminded of it five days a week, eight hours a day. Or if you make a play and it works, he may turn out to be a dud and you'll have to break it off. The worst scenario is your job being at risk.

High-Risk Men

1. **Men who give mixed signals.**

They oogle you, act seductive with you, but never ask you out. Some of these men may be playing a game of deception with women, and some are genuinely unaware of what they are doing. It may be that they are attracted, but at some level of consciousness they are fearful of becoming involved with you, or women in general, or, for example, women they work with. When things don't pan out, you may suffer needlessly from feelings of rejection, when, in fact, you were the victim of a deception, conscious or unconscious.

2. **The Himbo.**

He's always looking for a quick roll in the hay with no commitment or attachment of any kind. If you fall for this guy, you will get a quick affair and be abandoned almost as soon as he gets his pants back on.

3. **He's gay (but doesn't want you to know or hasn't come out of the closet).**

He has the signs or being receptive, but nothing romantic ever materializes. He'll definitely do lunch with you, but it'll never go any further.

4. **The Closet Attached Man.**

They're often receptive and very seductive, but they're already attached. They just don't let you know about their relationship or marriage, and you end up finding out from someone else.

5. **The Ambivalent Attached Man.**

He flirts like crazy but never follows through. He's in a relationship or married, but part of him wants out. He acts out his ambivalence by flirting with you and sending you double messages. He's crazy making because he runs hot and cold. Until he leaves his significant other, he is a very high-risk man.

Plan of Action

OK, you decide to roll the dice and take a chance. Life is a crap shoot. So, here's the plan, ladies.

STEP ONE: MAKE YOUR MOVE

Take very small steps. If they don't work, you've risked almost nothing and you won't feel so awkward around each other afterward.

If you already speak to him regularly, try a casual lunch invitation, perhaps with a work connection. "Hey, I'm starved. You want to come with me to _____ and talk about this while we eat?" If you don't regularly speak to him, try inquiring about what he does, and then, if he seems ready for it, do the casual lunch invitation.

Perhaps he's not a coworker but someone you're on a committee with or taking a class with.

"I was interested in what you were saying tonight. I'd like to ask you more about that. Do you have time for coffee?" Again, little risk, no pressure on him. He can do it or not do it, and it's neither a commitment if he does, nor a big rejection if he doesn't.

STEP TWO: THE CASUAL DATE

You're having lunch or coffee with him. Gently explore to find out how available he is. You know the standard techniques. "Oh, I don't mean to make you late for anything. Do you have someone waiting for you?" It's OK to be frank and ask directly if he has someone in his life. Just don't get upset if you find out he's taken.

Check out his reactions to you. Is he interested in you in a romantic or sexual way? Watch his body language. Does he gaze into your eyes when he speaks? Does he ever look at your body? Naturally, you're doing this automatically at the same time you're assessing his availability.

While you're doing all this, try to have an engaging conversation. You can use this as an opportunity to strengthen your connection with him. You can also review some tips in the "Dating Etiquette" chapter. And most importantly, enjoy yourself!

STEP THREE: IT'S UP TO HIM NOW

By having lunch or coffee and signaling your interest, you've advanced the relationship from zero to one. Now, leave it up to him to make the next move. You can encourage him to make the move ("I've really enjoyed this. It's so easy to talk to you"), but let him make it. He's got to invest, too. That's for his sake, as well as yours, and for the good of the relationship. He needs to feel a degree of ownership and control. If he's not ready to make the move, be patient for a while. He may come around in a few days. If not, then so be it. You tried.

The One-Time Situation

Here is where, in baseball terms, you get only one swing at the plate. You've gone to a lecture and he's the lecturer, or maybe another person there in attendance. You're in a limo getting a ride to the airport. You're visiting someone in the hospital and he works there. You like him. Maybe it's his looks. Maybe he says intelligent things. Or he just makes you laugh till tears run down your face. What do you do to get things rolling? Now remember what I said before about being aggressive. Here you have to be super-aggressive or you won't get a second shot.

Step One: Business Cards

Always, always carry a business card with you. If you must, put this book down right now and run out to your nearest printing store and have them make some up for you!

Step Two: Introduce Yourself

How you do this and what exactly you say depends, of course, on circumstances. "Hi, I liked your talk very much. Do you have a business card? Could I call you sometime to ask you some questions about (topics he spoke about in his "talk").

Or "Hi, My name is _____ . Here's my card. I notice you were as interested as I was in what he said tonight.

If it's OK, I'd be interested in comparing reactions sometime. Do you have a card?"

Or "You don't seem like the usual guys I get on this ride to the airport. Are you an actor or going to school or something like that?"

Step Three: Give Him Your Contact Number
In sales lingo, you're going to hand him your business card as you "close." In the event you don't have your card on you, give him your phone number instead.

Step Four: Get His Contact Information
Always, always, always, get his business card or phone number. This is even more important than him having your card or phone number. This way you don't lose out on any opportunities.

Step Five: Follow Up
If he takes your card and you still don't hear from him, call him. What the hell! You'll never see him again anyway. If he doesn't sound excited to hear your voice, then just talk a couple of minutes and get off. If he does sound happy to hear from you, talk a while and try to pin him down for a casual date. If he turns you down, at the very least you tried. Remember, you got to be in it to win it.

Chapter 15

He Drops You!
What's a
Girl to Do?

Renee was seeing Rob for one month when he suddenly announced he wouldn't be calling her anymore. Renee was totally taken by surprise because she thought they were having such a great time. Hurt and devastated, Renee called Rob afterward and yelled at him for leading her on. The next day she felt humiliated that she let him know how much he meant to her when he obviously didn't feel the same way. Renee deeply regretted how she handled Rob's decision to end their brief dating relationship.

Although dating is supposed to be a fun process of "getting to know you," the reality is it's filled with high expectations and dreams of walking down the aisle, in addition to deep longing for attachment and love. So, when a man unexpectedly drops you or ends a connection after only a few dates, it can be extremely upsetting and in some instances heartbreaking. Therefore, I think it's of utmost importance for you to handle being dropped with dignity, grace, and self-respect.

If you follow my ten suggestions you will be able to manage surviving a man's rejection with your self-esteem intact. You'll also be able to quickly emotionally restore yourself, so you can keep up your emotional strength to go out there again and keep dating. So, when a man tells you he doesn't want to date any further:

1. **Whatever you do, do NOT act like a victim.**

Do not cry, beg, grovel, hit him, or throw things at him. Don't threaten to harm yourself. The more extreme your threats and actions are, the more pathetic you look in his eyes. It's important to stay calm, because when you appear cool:

- The better you'll feel about yourself despite how horrible the situation is.
- He may regret his decision later on, and you don't want him to remember you as a psycho bitch.

- Also, he may be one of those seductive, exciting/rejecting dudes, and you don't want to gratify his sadism by showing him how injured you feel. Self-protection is the key here.

2. Find out why he is making this decision.

Speak logically. Counterpoint anything he says if it doesn't make any sense to you, and if you feel you can give him some insight into some emotional issue he may be struggling with. Remember not to act desperate no matter what . . . even if your heart is breaking.

3. The right time to fall apart . . .

When you're done talking to him and he is gone . . . only then can you fall apart. Go over to your best friend's house or call her up. Scream and carry on all you want, just don't do it in front of him.

4. After he's gone . . .

Do not talk with him anymore, unless he tells you he realizes he made a mistake and wants to reconcile and keep dating you.

5. Don't seek revenge.

Revenge makes you look desperate, lonely, and emotionally disturbed. Revenge is a way of staying attached. It never, never gets him back.

6. Don't try to get good closure.

There is no good closure. Even if you say everything you want, then you'll feel the pain of losing him again, and you'll need more closure. It's a vicious cycle. There's always pain when a relationship ends, and it's often emotionally messy. Your closure is the work you do to let go of him. You can work closure through with your therapist and/or friends.

7. Try, try, try not to obsess about him.

Obsessing about him after it's over is a way of avoiding facing the pain of your loss. Examining him and the situation over and over in your mind won't bring him back or get life to turn out the way you want.

So instead of ruminating, try to feel your emotions that are coming up. Mourn and grieve him and the future you wished for or dreamed of. The only way to really let him go is to embrace the painful feelings and then move through them. Obsessing about him is a way to avoid the emotional work you have to do.

If none of this works, snap a rubber band on your wrist when you think of him. Many women in my groups claim this works for them. Distract, distract, distract yourself. It's work but doable.

8. Don't stay friends with him.

Staying friends with a man who rejects you is often an excuse to somehow stay connected to him. It's sometimes a woman's inability to detach from a man who is not interested in having the kind of relationship that she wants that will continue to cause problems for her after the breakup. Why would you want to invest in staying friends with a man who has rejected you? Why aren't you insulted and angry at his lack of interest in reciprocating your feelings? Why do you want to subject yourself to hearing him talk about the new women in his life? Bottom line is, if a man doesn't want you the way you want him, why do you want a friendship with him?

9. Don't contact him.

Do whatever it takes not to contact him. Do not e-mail him, IM him, go to his house or his job, or call him. Each time you connect with him, it makes it more difficult to let go of him. The bond keeps re-cementing. The memory traces of him in your brain keep strengthening rather than eroding. That's why the saying "time heals all wounds" is true. The fewer memories you have of your ex, the easier it is to forget him. It's Mother Nature doing her work.

10. Start dating again.

Don't let the loser slow you down. Don't give him the power to stop you on your dating journey. Healthy women move on and let go. They don't stay in continual mourning. Just keep on truckin', girlfriend! NEXT!

Chapter 16

Men on Dating and Relationships

Often women want to know why men do the things they do and make the choices they make in terms of dating women and forming relationships. So, I decided to ask my round table of five men about this entire subject to help enlighten you, which, I hope, will result in your making better decisions and choices when dating and relating to men.

 In your opinion what constitutes a date?

Bob

A formal get-together between two people who are attracted to one another.

Donald

A "date" happens when a guy OR a girl (this is the twenty-first century) asks the other to do something "intimate" (going to Starbucks does not cut it). This can be drinks and dinner or could be going to a game or concert. Ultimately, there must be motive by the person who asked you out—either to have sex or explore the potential for a relationship.

Doug

A date is spending time with someone to whom you are attracted. It could be anything—dinner, a movie, or even watching TV together. So long as it is positive shared moments, it's all good.

Jerry

A date is when two people plan to get together. I don't think it has to be anything elaborate or going out to any place in particular. It's just the act to see one another or get together because there is some sort of mutual attraction there.

Tom

A date is a commitment by a man and woman to do something positive about starting or continuing the relationship. That's the key for me.

Is it a date when I chance to meet a woman at a lecture and we become strongly attracted to each other? No, that's lucky, but not a date. It happened to me, though. Met someone at a lecture. We started talking, and we were soon babbling away and laughing and falling in love. It was wonderful. It promptly led to a long relationship, but no wedding. The long period of intimacy allowed us to see the problems each of us brought to the relationship, yet lacked the maturity and genuine commitment to deal with.

 Describe your ideal date.

Bob

I have no bona fide "blueprint" or "prescription" for the ideal situation on a date. Ideally, I could only hope for a woman to be herself. Although I do prefer to avoid crowds and noise so we can communicate without too many distractions.

Donald

An "ideal date" depends on where you are in the relationship. However, in the early stages, it would be some cocktails at a "cool" place and then having an easygoing dinner (for instance, sushi or some Mexican). Afterwards, going out for a bit of "fun." The reader is probably wondering what "fun" comprises. This, to me, is exactly what makes or breaks a date. For instance, going out dancing or doing something where you can interact together—a place where you can interact and get the feel for someone. If it turns out to be a fun night, odds are strong for a sequel date.

Doug

I enjoy quiet, intimate settings, dinner out or in either of our apartments followed by a movie, snuggling, and massages—most of the time leading to kissing, fondling, then sex. That's not always the case, but any grouping of these is a good date for me.

Jerry

Good conversation. Physical chemistry. Not wondering how to end the date or when it will be over. One that ends in a way that makes me want to see the person again.

Tom

I'm talking here only about a first date. Having a good time in each other's company is key, no matter what activities we are doing on the date. We both must be enjoying the time and it has to be because of the other person, not just because it's a good movie or good dinner, etc. It's vital to my good time that she be enjoying herself as much—or pretty close, anyway—as I do. Overall, I feel a strong attraction to her and I sense she is attracted to me. At the end of the evening, there's a nice, warm kiss—it doesn't necessarily have to go further than that.

 What is one thing that would turn you off to a woman you start dating and maybe you would want to change about her?

Bob

If she was unnecessarily rude to people, or consistently acted as if she had some false sense of entitlement (a.k.a., a spoiled brat).

Donald

When she has a boyfriend and is seeing me on the side.

Doug

Usually someone who is pushy or demanding and possessive. Also, a big one for me is someone who is rude or obnoxious.

Jerry

Being too needy.

Tom

If she complains about me to others, either in front of me or not. I don't mean sharing with her girlfriend about some aspect of my personality that gives her a problem. I mean complaining for the sake of complaining—without seeking to understand or deal with the problem constructively.

 What makes you ask a woman out?

Bob

If something in her personality portrayed a uniqueness that makes her stand out as different.

Doug

Women who have great character/attitude and personalities, along with being physically attractive to me.

Jerry

I usually ask a woman out based on my first impression of her, which is usually because she's physically attractive to me.

Tom

In order for me to ask a woman out, I would have to see that she has interests in life beyond herself. If she's able to talk about a wide variety of subjects, such as current events, books, pop culture, I'm attracted to that. Of course, if she's kind of narrow in her interests yet extremely seductive as well, that's hard for me to resist. That doesn't happen that often, though.

The next big factor is the likelihood of her saying yes. It hurts to be rejected, so I would have to believe that she likes me and would be glad to go out with me.

Face and figure do play a role; my attention would initially be drawn to a woman with a pretty face and/or a good figure. However, if she doesn't get past the first two items above, I'm not going to ask her out.

 What would you consider more important, a woman's beauty or personality?

Bob

Personality, without a doubt.

Donald

A combination of both. There are many attractive women everywhere, but if they are shallow and narcissistic, they aren't any fun to be around. It's finding that combination of looks and personality that can bring true happiness. If you have both qualities: your guy is going to stick around.

Doug

Looks can only get you so far. Of course, looks are what I usually focus on, but ultimately, it's the woman's personality that really hooks me.

Jerry

They both carry the same weight for me, but if I had to give up a little more of one, I'd give up the beauty.

Tom

Personality—hands down! The most beautiful woman with the greatest body in the world gets to be a drag without a good personality. The fact is, you get used to the looks after a while and they don't mean that much anymore.

 What would make you break up with a woman?

Bob

It would have to be something very severe. I wouldn't invest my time with anyone that I wouldn't have great patience with. Betrayal would have me thinking long and hard about leaving her, but even that isn't set in stone. We are human and we do make mistakes that are often forgivable. It would depend on the severity of it.

Donald

If she thinks about herself all the time—I am gone. There is no "I" in team. A relationship is a team. And the team can be good and can get better and better over time. However, if she is constantly focusing on herself all of the time—the relationship is a loser.

Doug

If she is consistently belligerent or angry with me. Or if over time she proves to be uncaring and selfish and not willing to share emotions.

Jerry

I would seriously think of breaking it off with a woman if the relationship progressed and it became clear that we weren't emotionally at the same stage. If we're both moving in different directions, like if she wants a larger commitment and I'm not ready, then I would probably consider breaking up with her.

Tom

The main thing that would make me want to break up with a woman would be if we were not getting along well. What's the sense of being in a relationship with someone if you're constantly fighting?

Also, if I were to discover something about her that I don't think I can live with, such as a bad attitude, drug or alcohol abuse, excessive dependence, etc.

 Have you thought about what, if anything, would make you want to marry a woman?

Bob

I myself do NOT believe very strongly in the concept of marriage. It seems somewhat narrow-minded to me. Two people either love each other and stand by each other, or they do not. However, if marriage meant a lot to the woman I loved I would consider it. This is probably an oxymoron though, because I probably would not be attracted to a woman who's mode of thinking would lead her to covet the idea of marriage.

Donald

If she is both my best friend and my love interest, and if the relationship is ongoing and satisfying, then I would consider asking her to marry me.

Doug

If she possessed the best attributes: intelligence, beauty, wit, humorous, healthy sexual appetite, overall confidence, and artistic ability.

Jerry

I would most definitely consider marriage if I had the feeling that she and I could be compatible for the long run. I also find it important that we understand each other's ways of thinking, which would mean that we know how to approach each other and deal with difficult situations together. I guess that boils down to compatibility.

Tom

When she is enjoyable to be with, even when she's not at her best, demonstrates good partnership skills, and she shares the same basic life values.

 Do you expect a woman to pay for part of a date, or do you prefer to pay?

Bob

I prefer to pay.

Donald

What's next! Are women going to open doors for us!? Generally, men pay (especially on a first or second date). On occasion (after dating for a month), it is nice for the woman to pay for cocktails or movies and the man to pay for dinner. However, once again, men should be paying most of the time. No splitting!

Doug

I always pay, even if it's a friendly get-together. I feel better giving than to go halfsies with a date/friend.

Jerry

I always prefer to pay, even though at times I regret spending on a date. I personally think that it's a man's place in the early stage of the game to do so, but if I had financial problems and felt comfortable enough to tell her about it, then I would ask her to split it with me. Generally speaking, if I am with someone I end up paying unless she insists on taking a tab.

Tom

I prefer to pay, even though I know this is a practice based on a view of women as dependent on men and something of a prize for men to win. I believe in equality and that I should be just as much of a prize. Moreover, women today are often quite able to support themselves and do not need a man for that purpose. However, it's very difficult for me, as well as for most people, to overcome so many years of acculturation on this issue.

 How would you feel if you were dating a woman who makes more money than you?

Bob

This doesn't bother me. More power to her. I would actually be impressed if she was making a lot of money doing something she genuinely enjoyed doing.

Donald

No big deal. I actually think that is awesome.

Doug

Where do I sign up? I have done that and have no problem with that. I feel totally secure with myself. It is my experience that a woman with money knows exactly what she wants and is confident—that is sexy to me.

Jerry

This isn't an issue for me. In fact, I'd respect her more for it. The question is would I feel inferior to her. Never been in a position like that, but I would say that I'd have enough confidence not to heretofore, I would love it if my woman made more money than I did. Hell, it would motivate me to do and/or be more.

Tom

I say it doesn't matter, but I know that deep down it would bother me. Lots of acculturation to overcome. Would it stop me from continuing the relationship? Not if we enjoyed being together. If she were the kind of woman I am attracted to, we would be honest with each other about the issue and work out a way to handle it. That might well include me doing work on my assumptions and perceptions.

 Do you prefer dating a woman who makes more money than you or less money than you?

Bob

I have no preference. The thought in itself is a bit shallow and superficial as far as I'm concerned.

Donald

Not important. Money should not be the driving factor. Honestly, are you going to know how much someone is making on one or two dates? You may not know for quite longer. If you do, I would say that this is a warning sign because the guy or girl should have more game than to talk about how much he or she earns.

Doug

I would prefer someone who makes less money only because they might appreciate things more and be more open to new experiences, having had fewer opportunities. But that's from my personal experience— there are definite exceptions.

Jerry

More, of course. Sometimes I may feel that a woman with financial struggles may want to be with me for security or reasons other than "me." So if she is making more than me, it makes me feel like she wants to be with me just because of "me."

Tom

Same answer as for the previous question.

If you had to choose between dating a woman who had your ideal body type but a boring personality and a woman who had a great personality and who wasn't your ideal body type, who would you prefer dating?

Bob

I would prefer the great personality. People can get physically "in shape" a lot easier than they can reverse being a bore or a jerk. I would settle for neither, though. I want the "whole package" so to speak.

Donald

The girl with the ideal body type is going to get old and lose the looks eventually. Then imagine yourself with a flat soda for the rest of your life (yuck!). Honestly, I want the woman who has a great personality and who is fun.

Doug

It depends on what point I'm at in my life, as far as looking for someone. If I'm looking for a relationship, then personality is more important to me. But for just dating short-term, I'd have to go with looks, unless the woman's personality is unbearable.

Jerry

In most cases I wouldn't date a woman who didn't have my ideal body type, therefore not allowing me to get to know her personality. Great personality is important but doesn't supplement for a great body, especially in the beginning. Personality for the long run, for sure, though.

Tom

Not a moment of thought required here. I would unhesitatingly date the great personality.

Once I've had sex with a woman, my needs in that department are satisfied for the time being, and her physical charms no longer mean that much to me. If she's a nag or complainer or just boring, I soon lose interest in being close. Pretty soon, the relationship becomes purely sexual. I endure what I need to in order to get to have sex with her, and then find a reason to get away from her, either physically or mentally. Pretty soon, I'm not even interested in the sex.

 Do you find a woman more enticing if she is more challenging and unavailable (even while you are in a relationship with her), or a woman who is emotionally available and in to you and doesn't cause you any problems?

Bob

This is a no-brainer. A woman who is emotionally available and in to you is always favorable to an emotionally unstable drama queen who needs to be the center of attention and feeds off chaos. Drama queens usually attract guys who are emotionally disturbed themselves. Water usually seeks its own level.

Donald

Isn't it funny how life works?! My longest relationship was with a girl who was more challenging and unavailable. During those four years, she would be "on" sometimes and "off" sometimes. I guess just like being a drug addict, you become addicted to the highs and lows and all of the drama of the relationship. In looking back, we really do not need the drama. Thus, now that I am "clean," I would prefer to be with someone who is available.

Doug

I'd really have to go with the latter answer. I've had too many problems trying to explain and understand the "challenged" ones—it's way too exhausting and a waste of positive energy that could be used for bettering myself or another relationship.

Jerry

It's always more enticing at first when a woman is unavailable, but I am very aware that the feeling only gets you so far. For a long-lasting, successful relationship, I know that I need the availability, but the problem with availability is that it gets boring. While it's always nice to have a woman keep me on my toes, I guess it's not worth the cost of an unstable relationship. I guess the right balance of both would be ideal.

Tom

I have enough of my own problems so I don't need additional ones from a relationship that I have embarked on in order to gain more contentment and happiness in life. I am competitive in certain areas but not in love. The lower the hurdle, the better. Whether I am coming to see her after a great day or a lousy one, I want to have a soul mate, a partner, a friend—not another problem or challenge.

 Is age a factor for you at all in dating? Do you prefer a woman who is older or younger than you?

Bob

I have no definitive preference. It simply depends on where their head is (among other factors).

Donald

I prefer a younger woman.

Doug

I prefer to date a woman that looks younger than me. If anybody takes care of themselves, that is always an instant turn-on. I've dated women older than me who have better overall beauty than twenty-year-olds. It's all relevant to how much you care about yourself. To me, age is just a number, but some woman do have a genetic advantage over others. Just work with what you have and enjoy yourself.

Jerry

When I was younger, I preferred dating older women. Today, I'm thirty-two and don't think I want an older woman, but a mature woman is a must.

Tom

Hard to say. I don't think I've ever dated an older woman, but it's not because I'm opposed to it.

Women are like wine. It's not necessarily the age of the wine or the shape of the bottle or how pretty the label; it's how the wine tastes and makes you feel—how you experience it—that counts.

Would you consider getting involved in a relationship with a woman who already has children?

Bob

Probably, but not necessarily. Children bring LOTS more responsibility. It would have to be a unique situation for me to want the responsibility that comes with being a "parent" to a woman's child (or children).

Donald

I would not *not* consider it. It all depends on the situation.

Doug

Yes, it would affect my decision. I believe that I could never be that child's parent and would prefer to start my own family, if I would choose to involve kids with a relationship. Raising children is such an important role, which, I think, people don't take seriously enough. Children need stability.

Jerry

It could, but it wouldn't be the deciding factor.

Tom

When I was dating between marriages, most of the women I saw had children, some living at home with them. It didn't bother me at all. I enjoy children, so it was a plus rather than a minus. How would I feel about marrying such a woman? I would have had to be sure, if they were minor children, that their father would continue child support payments. At that time, I had two children of my own whom I was paying child support for.

I would also have had to be sure that any issues between the children and me were solvable with time. I think little boys are easier for the new man than little girls. Girls sometimes defend the place of the absent father by making the home as uncomfortable as possible for the new man. They remain aloof to the point of rudeness at times. That creates problems with Mom, which adds to the discomfort for the new man. This never happened to me, but I did experience some rudeness or coldness from girls.

Boys, in my limited experience, were always ready to welcome a new adult male, and sometimes quite joyously, particularly if their own father had been absent or otherwise neglectful.

 If you were very attracted to a woman but she was physically challenged or disabled, would you consider having a relationship with her?

Bob

Yes, but I would have to seriously consider her limitations and how drastically they would affect a potential relationship with her.

Donald

Yes.

Doug

It would really depend on the severity of the disability—there are many women out there with disabilities who are so wonderful and beautiful inside, but people won't look past the physical and meet the real person.

Jerry

Yes. I would.

Tom

Tough question to answer in the abstract. If we started as friends or even coworkers, and the relationship slowly bloomed, I wouldn't feel the pressure to make a commitment decision until long after the disability ceased to matter so much.

 How would you describe your ideal woman?

Bob

I don't think in terms of the "ideal" woman anymore. I believe that by putting unrealistic expectations on people, we limit our imaginations and sometimes miss out on certain beautiful (and mysterious) aspects of people whom we previously had no conception of. I can only look at kindness, creativeness, and intelligence as idealistic qualities that I would hope for a woman to have. Ideally, I would want her to be herself, not someone who is molded (and limited) by my personal imagination.

Donald

My ideal woman is someone who is cute, comfortable in her own skin, and fun to be around. She has lots of friends and has her "own life." She likes to work and play hard.

Doug

Intelligent, confident, physically fit, long hair, artistic in some way (music, art, etc.), caring and giving, funny/witty, with a sweet voice and personality. That's not asking for too much, is it?

Jerry

Hot, sexy, smart, successful, funny, social, confident, loving, and caring. Is there such thing?

 A woman has been dating a man for a year. Her biological clock is ticking and she wants to get married and have a family. However, the man shows no signs of wanting to take the relationship to the next step. How would you suggest she handle the situation?

Bob

She should either move on and find another man who has similar goals, or re-evaluate her own goals (or motives) of having a family.

Donald

Honestly, she needs to figure out if the guy is "all-in" or not. Relationships are gambles. If he is not a keeper, you need to move on to the next hand!

Doug

Lay down the law. Say, "I want a family and you are either up for the challenge or out on the curb!" Most people wait too long and waste too much time in a relationship without really getting to know the other person and getting what they need from them and the relationship. Make the leap or move on.

Jerry

Express to him what your needs are, and if he is incapable of fulfilling them, start seeing others. We must, as adults, have the ability to make these decisions without having the perfect answer or advice. Weigh the relationship and make the best decision you can as a mature responsible adult.

Tom

Tough without knowing who the guy is. Why hasn't he made more of a commitment after a year? What's with him? Is he scared of commitment? Is he just using you for easy sex? Could you be part of a harem? Maybe he's just scared of making the first move for fear that you'll reject him.

Best advice I can give: sit him down, let him relax, and try to open up the channel of communication by telling him how much you like him and enjoy being with him. See his reaction and go from there.

 A woman is dating a man who will only see her during the week and not on the weekends. She likes him, but she's not sure how to handle the situation. How would you advise her?

Bob

Accept it or move on to something else. He's probably married anyway.

Donald

86 him! If you ever worked in a restaurant—you know what that means.

Doug

Find someone else who will spend time with you on the weekend or find someone who will see you whenever you want. Unless this person is so amazing that you are willing to lose out on portions of your life, you can find someone that will be there when you want/need them.

Jerry

Chances are he doesn't want a commitment. So, she should keep seeing him only if she understands that she may be putting herself in a situation in which she's not getting what she needs from the relationship. Women should stop trying to change things and, rather, focus on accepting things the way they are and figure out if they can gain something from it or not. Example: If she knows that all he wants is a weekday lover, or not getting exclusive, then she should accept it and try and meet someone else on the weekend and keep him on the side like he keeps her. Or if she can't handle it, end it and move on. Don't kill yourself over it.

Tom

If he's not telling, then it's probably something he doesn't want you to know about. My guess: he's married and tells his wife he has clients to see at night. Another guess: he's serving a weekend sentence. Still another guess: he has a girlfriend who is a flight attendant and can only see him on weekends. Most optimistic guess: he's getting a degree part-time and he has to be on campus on weekends.

Why don't you ask him to accompany you to a weekend event? He's got to give some reason, even if it's only, "Oh, I'm busy that weekend." In that case, keep asking him about going with you to a weekend event. He can't very well keep saying that he's busy without offering at least some explanation. If it's a wife or a girlfriend, he's probably got a well-rehearsed lie to tell you, but you may be able to see through it. Anyway, it doesn't really cost anything to ask, and it may yield some valuable information.

 Where and how you would you advise women to meet men who are seriously looking for a relationship?

Bob

Go to places that you have interest in. Water seeks its own level. Like-minded people have a greater chance of meeting each other at events that they both have interest in. In other words, if you are a rocket scientist, it is very unlikely that you will find an intellectual woman hanging out at the corner bar at happy hour.

Donald

I constantly have female friends complain to me that they never meet anybody. Sound familiar?! I then observe them when we are out at a bar or restaurant. The problem: they are not putting themselves out there! Ladies, not all men are smooth and have the "game" to pick you up. You have to help us and give us some hints that you are interested.

In any event, I would suggest going to parties (because you can play that "two degree of separation" thing). I think the more parties you go to, the higher your odds of meeting someone who is a friend of a friend and may have similar interests as you too.

Doug

There are serious men everywhere. My advice is to just be honest and open and direct with anyone you meet and just communicate what you are looking for—men love directness. I believe that there are no women or men out of each other's league—everybody is fair game.

Jerry

Tough one. Choose activities that will get you out there mingling with others who have the same interests. Or why not try going online? Tons of people are meeting that way every day, and it increases your odds of finding someone you're compatible with. If you're looking for something serious, stay away from bars and clubs.

Tom

I would begin by doing whatever I could to build my circle of friends and acquaintances, and let them know what I was looking for. I believe that a very high percent of marriages occur through introductions by a third person.

Next, I would try to loosely profile the kind of man I was looking for and go to places where such a man would be likely to go. Intellectuals go to bookstores, libraries, lectures, evening courses, study groups; aesthetes are likely to be found at concerts, art galleries, museums; regular Joes can be found at the ballpark; men who are trying to live better lives join self-help groups of one kind or another; politically oriented men volunteer to make calls and help with mailings for candidates; religious types are found in houses of worship; and so on.

Getting involved in some kind of group that meets regularly helps: you usually get to know the men in the group somewhat before deciding whether you want to date them.

No gold-plated guarantees that any of these strategies will work every time with every woman, but I believe they do improve your odds considerably over simply staying home and waiting for the telephone to ring.

 If you could give advice to a woman on how to get a man to fall in love with her, what would you tell her?

Bob

Be yourself. That is the only advice that can possibly be given that could produce genuine results. If you create a false image of yourself that is crafted merely to "snare" a man, you will be setting yourself up for a miserable life with him once he discovers the "real you." You should look for a man whom you could fall for, rather than worrying about whether or not he will fall in love with you. You can't force or trick anyone into falling in love and staying in love with you.

Donald

No answer.

Doug

Always be there for them, show confidence and self-esteem. Always talk about problems when they arise and before it's too late; find out what he really likes and pretend that he's the center of the universe, and he's hooked. Oh, and great sex helps.

Jerry

You can't make someone fall in love with you, so don't try to do that. Just be yourself and let him do the rest himself. It is a big turnoff to see a woman try too hard to impress. It's not your duty to make him fall in love with you. Ask yourself this, did he do anything to make you fall in love with him? Probably not. Then do just as much.

Tom

I think that falling in love is a different experience for men and women. For women, I think it's a kind of adoration, a deeply visceral attraction which makes the man the be-all and end-all for her. She loves the whole idea of the relationship, including the changes in her life that she sees resulting from it. She fantasizes about introducing him to her girlfriends and family. She imagines the apartment they will live in; she practices signing her married name; she thinks about the children they will have. All this, of course, starts right after the first date if she likes the man.

For men, it's much more pedestrian. In the distant past, when brides were virgins, falling in love for men was, at least in part, a way of experiencing sexual desire. Nowadays, a man doesn't necessarily fall in love with the woman he proposes to: having had sex with her on numerous occasions precludes this feeling. He cares greatly about her, likes being around her, depends on her emotionally, has life values that match hers, has life plans that agree with or at least do not conflict with hers, and she doesn't have any habits, personal problems, or mannerisms he can't stand. It's a plus if he also likes her friends and family.

So, how does a woman get a man to fall in love with her? The goal shouldn't be making someone fall in love with you. It's about compatibility. If you're aiming for anything, you should aim at being the kind of woman he likes being around. If he misses you when you're not around, you've come most of the way. Missing you is a sign of emotional dependence on you, which is good for him to have. The more fun he has with you—either in bed or out, preferably both—the better you're doing. If sex between the two of you feels good and if you're both feeling happy and loving afterwards, it's working.

As for out-of-bed experience, be a good friend. That's the most important thing. Listen when he needs a sympathetic ear; a warm hug is better than advice. Also, be open to trying new things together. He will appreciate your going to the game with him, even if you're not into sports. That tells him that he matters to you. Likewise, he should be willing to try new things with you.

Work on your companionship, too. You want him to enjoy his time with you. If he is reasonably well rounded and interested in the world outside himself (why else would you want a relationship with him?), you can talk to him about many of the same things you talk to your girlfriends about. Explore to see if there are other activities of mutual interest. Even if he doesn't do anything except work, eat, and sleep, he might like some of the things you do. You don't know until you try.

 Why do men say they are going to call and then don't call?

Bob

Sometimes men say they will call a woman just to avoid the uncomfortable moment when she asks, "When will you call me?" It is an easy way to avoid confrontation.

Donald

They have a girlfriend or they are seeing someone. If they are available—trust me—they will call. Then the ball is in your court!

Doug

The men that eventually do call are playing the wait three days to call her game, which is supposed to make it seem like he is not desperate.

Jerry

It's either 'cuz they didn't care for her that much or 'cuz they were too nervous and procrastinated so long that it turns into never.

Tom

I never did this. If I knew I wasn't going to want to see her again, I wouldn't say anything except maybe that I was glad to have met her or that I had a nice time. Something that says not to expect to hear from me.

Don't know for sure why men do this, but I can guess at some reasons. Some guys just aren't sure and want to see what develops over the next week or so. Maybe they'll meet someone they like better and maybe not, in which case it's good to have you as a backup. For other guys, they might do it just to avoid an unpleasant goodbye scene. Still others might not want you to feel rejected, at least not all at once.

What would make you not call a woman again after you've gone on a date with her?

Bob

Bad chemistry is the number one reason. If the chemistry just isn't there, then there is no reason to see her again. If you don't "click" on the first date, then it's not worth pursuing.

Donald

I'm not asking for your number unless I plan to call you. If afterward I'm feeling there's no connection, I'll find a way to let the woman know that. Once again, just like poker, every hand is not a good starting hand and you just have to throw it after a bit.

Doug

I think the biggest issue I have is a woman with no personality at all or one with a bad attitude/personality. Some women have had bad dating experiences/relationships and they bring that baggage along with them. This is a total red flag for me. If I'm on a date with a woman who is complaining about her past dates or relationships, I might try to tell get her to open up about it and then let it go, but if she keeps it up, I'd be tempted not to pursue her further.

Jerry

Shallow, bland . . . just not intriguing enough both physically or intellectually.

Tom

There could be many reasons. For me, most often, it was a strong feeling I got that the chemistry was not working and probably never would. Maybe she came across as too traditional for me, never thinking about anything much beyond family and home. She might be great for a traditional man who is looking only for a woman to manage the home and free him up to do what he likes. Sometimes women sent me vibes, consciously or unconsciously, that I was not the type they were looking for. On occasion, I had one-date-only relationships with women who revealed very serious personality problems. I was simply not willing to take on such problems.

 What would cause you not to call a woman you had sex with (so that it essentially turns into a one-night stand)?

Bob

Bad chemistry, once again. Also, she would have to be extremely annoying for me not to call (but I guess not too annoying to have sex with).

Donald

I think it would be some really bad behavior or personality flaw that would get to me. Most of the time, I get to know someone enough to understand the type of person they are or what they are capable of before I sleep with them.

If it happens to be someone I just picked up and I just met, then I would have to say it would be a shitty personality/rude behavior, no manners, or, even more basic, bad sex.

Jerry

If I don't call her after we've had sex, it's because I have no further interest in her.

Tom

For me, sex might occur when the woman felt desperate and wanted to jump-start the relationship. (An appropriate term for this behavior.) I couldn't say no, but once out of her home, I felt even guiltier so that I wanted to put as much distance as possible between the two of us.

Chapter 17

The Men You're Attracted To

"Why do I keep falling for men who can't meet my needs?" "Why do I keep falling for men who won't stick around?"

These are some of the most common questions I get from women. Sure, sometimes it's bad luck or poor karma, but that's not always the main issue. As you've learned from this book, it may have to do with the choices you make about the type of man you engage with.

Think back over your past relationships, and chances are you'll see striking similarities in the types of men you've dated. How many times have you chosen the same type of guy, even when you promise yourself that you'll never be attracted to a man like your last boyfriend ever again?

What's even more interesting is that even if you're choosing "good men," it's possible that your selections are still not the right men to bring you long-term happiness in a relationship.

A woman will often have an ideal of a man who turns her on. If she dates a man who isn't romantically stimulating enough, she perceives him as less than ideal and dismisses him, sometimes throwing away a potentially healthy relationship that could have had a future.

Many women get hurt due to choices based on their romantic ideals and then complain that "I can't go through this again. I want a different kind of relationship that doesn't lead to pain."

Becoming more aware of your judgment of men will help increase your chances of getting the relationship you want and lessen the possibility of your getting hurt, rejected, and/or disappointed.

So how do we choose the men we are attracted to?

The general consensus among most personality theorists is that the psychosocial interactions between children and caregivers play a significant role in determining whom you romantically and sexually desire.

So, whomever we love (mother, father, caretaker) and are loved by as young children becomes imprinted in our minds. These imprints cause us to be sexually and romantically attached to certain people who match our imprints. Object-relations theorists believe that it's the "entire relationship" with whomever we love (mother, father, caretaker) that gets imprinted in our minds. We then become attached to and repeat the way we related and were related to by our parents or caretaker.

This has very little to do with physical attraction, but psychologically, it's nearly a perfect fit. Research psychologists Money and Perper use the term "templates of human behavior" in referring to the object of the individual sexual arousal. Perper believes that such templates are not encoded but derive from developmental processes, including genetic regulation, neural development, and later neurophysiological construction of the image of the desired other. Money describes love maps as the development of the sexual objects one selects. He sees these as derived from schemata implanted on the brain and implemented by environmental input before age eight.[1]

Bottom line is the men you find sexually and romantically desirable have been wired in your brain since you were a little girl. It's a wild notion, isn't it?

However, it's important to keep in mind that if someone has had very upsetting experiences in their childhood, it will affect their judgment of men as an adult woman. The feelings that get triggered from trauma include anxiety, anger, rage, fear, panic, and stress. If women experienced these emotions on any kind of frequent basis as a child, when they are re-experienced as an adult as a result of being with a man that's unavailable or abusive, they feel familiar and are acceptable to her.

She may therefore feel compelled to re-enact her childhood experience with a man who she knows on an unconscious level will play out her old drama with her. The father of psychology, Freud, referred to the urgent need to repeat trauma as "repetition compulsion." So, in addition to its familiarity, she may also feel the need to "repeat" the past because she thinks she can undo the damaging experience by going through it again as an adult. In other words, if she can get an unavailable, rejecting man to become available and loving, she's changed history. She's undone the upsetting experience. Unfortunately, this rarely happens. She usually ends up being hurt again, emotionally injuring herself even more.

Some women feel so deeply wounded by the past they will not risk closeness with a man even though they crave deep connection. So, a woman may try to get involved but then choose an unavailable man she can blame for his inability to connect, thereby not gambling true intimacy.

Dee, an attractive thirty-three-year-old hairdresser, came to see me to try to find out why she had a pattern of getting involved with men who were initially seductive but always ended up disappointing her.

She reported that her mother suffered from a chronic heart condition and was often not physically or emotionally available to her. Occasionally her mom was hospitalized, but a great deal of time she was just resting. Dee remembers always being surrounded by babysitters and her mother's nurses. Her father, an insurance salesman, was physically unavailable because he worked long hours to pay for all the child care and medical bills.

Dee threw herself into her schoolwork, trying to be the good obedient daughter and not make more problems for her parents. Often she stayed with her aunt, who would help take care of her. When she turned eleven, her cousin William, who was four years older, started to tease her unmercifully. Not wanting to cause any problems, she didn't tell her mother or father and endured his torment until she was old enough not to have to stay at her aunt's house anymore.

Now, as a grown woman, Dee wonders if her poor judgment in men is due to her physically and emotionally unavailable father and mother, or to her abusive male cousin.

Do you have a pattern of the men you're attracted to?

To better understand your choices of men, let's take a look at your past by doing the following proactive writing exercise. Take your time and fill out the answers to each question.

1. **Write down the names of the men you've been in relationships with (serious or casual) until now.**

2. **Write down the names of men you've been attracted to and have not been in a relationship with.**

3. **If you have pictures of any of these men, get them out where you can see them.** Take a look at them and see if there are any physical features they all have in common. Do these physical features resemble anyone in your childhood?

4. **Look at the pictures and/or names and answer the following questions for each man.**

   - How old was he when you were involved or knew him?
   - What kind of job or profession did he have?
   - Was he ambitious or an underachiever?
   - What kind of childhood did he have? Was there trauma in his childhood?
   - How available was he? Was he married, single, dating other women, divorced, separated, bisexual?
   - What was your initial reaction when you first met?
   - How did he act to you when you first met?
   - When you first met, who was the pursuer?
   - Were you attracted to him right away, or did you become attracted after you got to know one another?
   - If you weren't attracted right away, at what point did you change your mind?
   - Did your feelings for him change over time? If they did, what was the time line?
   - Were you attracted to his potential, or to the person he really was?
   - Who ended the relationship: you or him?
   - Was it painful for you when it ended?
   - How quickly did you recover from the end of the relationship?
   - Do you still think about him?
   - Was he capable of having a relationship?
   - Did he want a relationship?

- How did he treat you during the relationship or while you knew him?
- Was he abusive?
- Was he nurturing?
- Was it a healthy relationship?
- Could you see yourself marrying him?

5. **What did all of these men have in common?**

6. **What feelings or behaviors did each man provoke in you?**

Utilize your answers to try to determine how you make your choices in men and how you can improve your dating process. Yvonne, a forty-eight-year-old stockbroker with an Ivy League education, started to do some self-exploration because she was hitting midlife and was embarrassed to admit that she had never been in a long-term relationship.

After reviewing her past relationships, Yvonne realized that every man she got involved with was unavailable. Two of her most memorable relationships were with men who said they weren't ready for a commitment. Even though she had some good times with them, in both cases the relationship went nowhere. Most of the dates consisted of sex, drinking, hanging out in her apartment, and occasionally going out to a bar or restaurant, but neither of these connections really turned into a viable relationship where she could say they were indeed a couple.

In filling out the answers to the questions on the previous pages, she realized she had a pattern of only dating men who were exceptionally good-looking. None of the men she became involved with were very ambitious or successful. In fact, most of them were still "finding themselves" or drifters. She couldn't imagine depending on them for anything substantial. In general, they were pretty adolescent in their thinking.

Yvonne also noticed that she was often the initiator. She had a tendency to run after them regardless of their interest in reciprocating her feelings. She didn't have the patience to see how or if a man was interested in her. Men occasionally pursued her, but she usually wasn't attracted to them. Yvonne liked to be the picker!

Ten-Step Program to Improve Your Choices of Men

1. Observe Emotionally Healthy Men

When you meet men in your general course of life (not necessarily to date or have a romantic relationship with), observe them. Do they possess any of the following positive characteristics?

- Nurturing
- Kind
- Committed to their children
- Committed to their marriages
- Stable
- Consistent
- Reliable
- Not exploitive
- Not sadistic

Take notes. Internalize them. It's never too late to start new imprints on your mind.

Dee, the woman from the first case study in this chapter, reported that she had several emotionally strong men in her life who could be role models: two coworkers, her dentist, and a neighbor. They were loyal to their wives and children, weren't addicted to drugs, had jobs and homes, and were reliable, stable, and kind. She thought about these traits and said she would try to prioritize them in her new choices in men.

2. Understand Your Past

Again, try to understand your childhood and how it affects your choices of men.

Dee understood that it was her parents' unavailability and her emotionally abusive cousin who might have caused her to develop not the best skills in selecting men to date and become involved with.

3. Become More Aware

A big step in changing is self-awareness. So work on becoming more aware of the type of men you are attracted to and why. Understand the repetitive and predictive patterns in your relationships. Become an observer of your own behavior.

Dee became aware that she was primarily attracting men who were very charming, self-absorbed, and unavailable, with a good rap. Dee realized that her expectations of men were very low, which resulted in her choosing men who were not nurturing, generous, or capable of offering her anything substantial. Only an occasional good time.

4. Work Through Your Emotional Wounds

As I discussed in Chapter 12, it helps to work through your emotional wounds with a therapist or people in your support system. Although therapy can take a lot of time, energy, and even money, it's healthier and more productive than re-enacting your childhood trauma over and over.

Dee committed to once-a-week psychotherapy sessions. She attended CODA (Codependents Anonymous) meetings faithfully. She also had several friends she spoke to on a regular basis

5. Accept Responsibility

Accept the responsibility of your present-day choices in men and the repetitive qualities of your behavior. It is when you own up to actions that are self-defeating that you can then make decisions on how to change.

Dee accepted her part in selecting men who weren't good candidates for a long-term relationship. She was willing to commit to doing the hard emotional work to change.

6. Know When You're Vulnerable

When you are making choices in men, know the times you are most vulnerable. For instance, if you're PMSing, or having problems on the job or an argument with your mother, you may not be at your best in terms of making sound, healthy choices.

Dee was feeling insecure about her health and her job. She knew that these problems resulted in her feeling especially needy and she would cling to any man who was receptive regardless of his capacity for a healthy relationship. When she was this vulnerable, all she could think of was lessening her anxiety.

7. Gather Information about Relationships

Read as much as you can about relationships. Get books from the library. Spend time in bookstores browsing around. Read book reviews in magazines and newspapers. Ask your friends for recommendations. You can also watch TV shows that can be full of information, with couples counseling occurring as you and the studio audience watches. Workshops are also helpful and enlightening.

Dee read as many books as she could on the subject of relationships and self-growth. She also asked for book recommendations from her friends at CODA.

8. Don't Be So Impulsive

Before you decide to spend time with a man, stop and think. Be mindful of the kind of man he is. Think of the consequences if he's one of your prototypes; that hasn't been the best choice for you in the past. Consider the possible outcome rather than just impulsively getting involved.

Dee became more selective about the men she decided to spend time with. Rather than just dating any man who asked her out, she would discuss the men she met with people in her support group and in therapy.

9. Be Open-Minded

Rather than pigeonhole yourself to a certain blueprint of a man, be open to the possibility of a different type of man. If you are more open-minded, there will be more men available for you to date!

Dee stopped only dating men she was initially very drawn to. She was now open to getting to know men she didn't necessarily feel attracted to. If she didn't feel bells go off on the first date, she'd still go out with him another few times and give him more of a chance.

10. Re-evaluate

Re-evaluate what you want in your relationship with a man. What your goals are will have an effect on your choices of men to relate to. If you're very interested in getting married, you have to take into account a man's emotional capacity for a long-term relationship; decide whether he's stable and reliable, and can earn a living. If you're just looking for fun, sex, or occasional companionship, then perhaps these qualities are not a priority.

Dee decided at this juncture of her life that she would like to have a partner to raise a family, and share financial responsibilities. She felt that it was hard being single and always depending on herself. She decided that her values about men would have to change; chemistry and butter-flies could no longer be the deciding factors.

Chapter 18

Improving Your "Assessment of Men" Skills

In addition to being aware of how your past affects your choices in men, it's also important to sharpen your current assessment skills so that you can accurately size up the men you date, or are interested in dating. If you keep choosing men who are immature, damaged, unavailable, or emotionally incapable of going beyond the third date, you will never achieve success in having a healthy long-term relationship. So here are ten general signs to look out for.

1. Is He Emotionally Available?

Some men are just not available. They could be married to a woman, and in some cases married to God. Some men are even married to their pathology. In other words, they're completely attached to their emotional problems and have absolutely no interest in changing. For instance, a man is afraid of abandonment, so he compulsively rejects the woman he falls in love with. His actions are usually unconscious and compulsive, stemming from his psychological issues to protect himself from getting hurt and damaged again, like when he was a little boy.

Another form of emotional unavailability is a man who has addiction problems—drinking, drugging, gambling, promiscuity—that he doesn't want to give up. The high from blackjack, drugs, or womanizing is more exciting and important than the boredom of a solid, stable, and committed relationship.

Some men are just plain scared of intimacy. They find relationships with women mysterious, scary, and threatening. They're emotionally unavailable because they end up distancing or ultimately running away.

Some men are committed to bachelorhood and have no interest in ever marrying.

The bottom line is that trying to have a relationship with a man who's emotionally unavailable is like swimming against the tide or trying to draw water from an empty well.

If having a long-term relationship is your goal, he's not the man for you.

2. "Boys in Men's Clothing"

There are some men who are very charming, fun, and sexy but unfortunately are also very immature, self-absorbed, and emotionally young. They are in essence "boys in men's clothing." They're like little toddlers wanting to be emotionally fed by their girlfriends/wives/mamas. Except they no longer cry for baby bottles filled with milk or Similac. Now, as physically grown men they want attention, love, sex, money, meals, and general fulfillment of all their emotional, physical, and sexual needs.

Basically, they want to see you at their convenience, when they feel like it, when they're in the mood for you, when it's good for them. It's always on their terms. Your needs or requests don't count. They can't tolerate demands, responsibility, commitment, or, God forbid, marriage. It's like putting a cross in front of a vampire. These are boys, not men.

Hanging out with them can be a hoot. They're often great company. They're terrific if you feel like reliving your adolescence, but if you're looking for a partner in a solid marriage with whom to build a future, sticking with a "boy in man's clothing" is setting yourself up for failure. Big time. I suggest you keep shopping.

3. Can He Sustain a Relationship?

Some men can start a relationship but can't sustain one. They have the ability to attach, often initially pursuing the women they're interested in.

However, they don't have the inner resources to tolerate all the feelings that come up in a long-term relationship—anger, love, fear, loss, frustration, disappointment. Fear of abandonment is also a biggie for them.

Bottom line, a man who can't sustain a relationship is the ultimate "exciting/rejecting lover." He seduces a woman into falling for him only to drop her like a hot potato. Sometimes he just disappears and other times he provokes her to dump him by acting outrageously horrible.

Unfortunately, the only way for you to find out about his capacity to be in a relationship for the long haul is to date him and see what he does as time passes. However, you can try to ask him about his past relationships with women. If they're mostly short-lived or chaotic—filled with breakups and makeups—then your days as a couple are probably numbered.

4. Can You Trust Him?

Men who provoke women to distrust them are often mysterious, secretive, and elusive, and have lied to them before.

A woman involved with a man she can't trust is often anxious about whether she's being "played," or consumed with thinking about whether he's lying to her or not. No matter how much she loves him, it's a life of hell and usually doesn't work. It's very emotionally draining and can cause a woman to become distracted from other healthy parts of her life such as her career and children.

However, before you throw in the towel, make sure that your inability to trust him is not your own "lack of trust" issues stemming from a traumatizing childhood or bad experience with men from your past. However, more often than not, this is not the case. I've found that men who are up-front, stable, and reliable do not usually induce feelings of distrust in their partners, even if the woman had severe trauma in her childhood or as an adult.

5. He Must Be Accountable

When you're in a relationship with a man, he must be accountable for his actions and words. If not, it will be almost impossible for the relationship to deepen and grow.

What does it mean to be accountable? When he says or does something that upsets or hurts you and you tell him, he must be able to own what he said or did.

He doesn't put it back on you and say "It's your problem" or "You're too sensitive." He has the emotional capacity to hear what you're saying and makes the effort not to say or do it again.

He takes responsibility for his behavior. If he acts seductive in the "getting to know you," pre-dating stage, he owns that he is sexually attracted to you and is flirting. He doesn't put it back on you and make you feel like you're going crazy or it's all your imagination.

Some men absolutely refuse to acknowledge that they are wounding or upsetting a woman. This kind of man wants to be completely accepted for who he is unconditionally. His way of thinking is, if you don't like what he says or does you just have to deal with it.

Men like this are almost impossible to have a healthy relationship with because not only is he dismissive and insensitive to your feelings, he's often out of touch with himself. The worst of it is your emotional needs don't get met.

6. He Must Be Able to Tolerate Your Limits and Boundaries

A man you're going to have a relationship with has to be able to honor your limits and boundaries. If he doesn't call when he says he will or is chronically late, and you tell him that he has to be more punctual and considerate of your time by calling when he says he will, he must go along with your limits and boundaries. If he can't, he's not a good prospect for a serious relationship. Some men are very emotionally limited and just don't have the capacity to tolerate other people's limits, which could leave you banging your head against the wall trying to change him.

7. He's Got to Want to Be in a Relationship

If the man you're attracted to does not want to be in a relationship, stay clear of him.

Don't be grandiose enough to think that you're special and will be the one to turn him around. You'll just waste a ton of precious time and most likely will end up getting hurt and possibly humiliated. Listen to what he's telling you if the man you're into says one of the following:

- "We can have a good time for now but there's no future."
- "I never want to get married."
- "I'm not looking for a relationship."
- "I've been celibate for spiritual reasons for three years now. I'm not interested in having a romantic relationship with a woman."
- "Relationships don't work."

Hanging out with a man who doesn't want to be in a relationship is setting yourself up for failure to find love and the relationship of your dreams.

8. Make Sure He's Consistent

Consistency is very important. If a man keeps changing his mind about you and the relationship, it can drive you batty. He's into you, then he's not into you. He wants a relationship, then he doesn't want a relationship. The type of man who can't make up his mind is an Ambivalent Man. As I described in my book *The Committment Cure*, the Ambivalent Man is "struggling with a profound sense of confusion that causes him to repeatedly sabotage romantic relationships or potential romantic relationships that could have otherwise been healthy and lasting."

To make use of the *Sex and the City* example one last time, Mr. Big is a classic example of an Ambivalent Man. Every time he becomes deeply involved with Carrie, he provokes a breakup. He's a great boyfriend and then he starts to distance. It's great television, but in real life this kind of inconsistent behavior is mind-boggling and emotionally draining, adding chaos to your life.

Unfortunately, the only way you will find out if he has problems with consistency is by dating him and seeing what he does. The first signs of highly ambivalent behavior could be the time to bail if confusing men are not your thing!

9. Can He Have a Relationship?

Some men are great to go out with. They're fun, romantic, charming, and reliable; they may even take you to nice places. The problem is they can't go beyond dating because they're looking for the perfect woman. Despite his own shortcomings (lack of money, unattractive), he'd rather remain single than commit to a woman who doesn't meet his own, often unrealistic expectations.

When a man who can't have a relationship dates a woman who's mainly interested in him, he starts to devalue her in his mind, spoiling the potential relationship by ending it or somehow getting the woman to break it off. Sometimes this process starts because she does something wrong that upsets him. He doesn't have the capacity to endure anger, disappointment, or another human being's imperfections, which is necessary in order to have a long-term relationship. Any romantic connection with a man who can't have a relationship is often short-lived.

10. He Has to Be Very Interested in You

If you're more interested in him than he is in you, it's not going to work, unless you're looking for a one-sided relationship. So make sure he's "very interested" before you get too attached. If you feel you're the pursuer and you're doing most of the initiating and emotional work, then he's not a good prospect for a long-term boyfriend or husband.

You can determine this by how often he calls you and wants to see you. If you get together less than once a week, forget it. He's definitely not that interested. It's also not a good sign if he only wants to see you during the week and not on the weekend.

If you just want to be his Tuesday-night fling, or if you want to be a woman he just sees at his convenience, then go for it. But if a long-term, exclusive relationship with a future is your goal, you must find a man who's "highly interested" in you.

Chapter 19

Tips on Dealing with Difficult Men

Here are some guidelines to help you emotionally protect yourself when dating men who have difficulties with relationships.

Change Your Phone Number

If you're trying to end a relationship with a man who is ambivalent or traumatizing you, then changing your phone number is a way for you to set firm limits and boundaries. There's nothing wrong with it, and, in fact, I suggest doing this if you have difficulty saying no to him. Also, you won't have to know or wonder whether he's trying to call you.

Talk Up!

Don't just take everything a man says to you at face value. If he comes up with a ridiculous reason or excuse for what he says or does, then say something. Don't set a precedent that you're a pushover. Let him know from the first date on that you're not a fool and that you have a mind of your own.

His Reality Isn't Your Reality

His reality may be a case he builds up to support his fear of commitment. For instance, he tells you it's better to date more than one person at a time or it's better to see each other on Sunday night rather than Saturday night. That's his opinion! You don't have to agree with him. Stick to your own reality.

Don't Let Him Downgrade the Relationship

If you've been dating exclusively and he wants to start dating other people, don't do it! Why would you anyway? Aren't you insulted that he doesn't want to have sex just with you anymore? His changing the nature of the relationship might mean that he met another woman or just isn't that interested in you or can't sustain a relationship. It's a waste of your time and will end up traumatizing you. Cut your losses and leave.

Doting on Him Won't Make Him Commit to You

Catering to a man or being his "love slave" (cooking for him, doing his laundry, giving him money) just makes you look codependent, unless he is reciprocating all your giving behavior. It's human nature to take advantage of people. So make sure that you're not setting yourself up to be exploited and used.

Don't Tolerate "Partial" Relationships

What are partial relationships? They include the following:

- You only see him during the week, never on the weekends
- A relationship that never goes anywhere
- He's involved with other women
- He only wants to see you when he is in the mood, at his convenience

Partial relationships are a way for him to get his needs met (sex, companionship, etc.) without his having to deal with his anxiety or issues about commitment. It's nothing but a compromise, and you get the raw end of the deal.

Stop Analyzing Him

I know he's an orphan, his mother left him when he was three, his wife cleaned him out, yada, yada, yada. Although it's sad and your heart goes out to him, if he dumped you or sees other women behind your back, his traumas are no reason to accept his bad, unloving treatment of you. The damage he incurs by other people in his past could be targeted toward you if it goes untreated. Although it is beneficial to understand the reason behind the inconsistent, rejecting behavior, if you use it to rationalize his bad treatment of you, you're setting yourself up for a big waste of a lot of precious time, and all on a man who's just not going to come through for you.

If a man is in a deep, committed relationship with you and it has a future, then it's appropriate to feel sorry for him and be empathic and understanding about his traumatic past. However, if he's hurting or traumatizing you, refer him to a shrink and wish him luck.

Know When to Cut Your Losses

I understand how much you may want to be in love and how much you adore the man you're seeing, but if he starts playing head games with you and is not genuine and authentic about wanting a serious relationship with you, consider the following:

- Remember that you will squander time, which can be detrimental and even self-destructive if you are in your childbearing years and want a family.
- Every breakup is a trauma, so the longer you stay with him, the longer it will take you to recover.

If a man breaks up with you and wants to just stay friends or have a partial relationship, the relationship will most likely not go anywhere or completely deteriorate. Get out! Drop him! Don't let him waste your time, traumatizing you for the next man who's out there, who may be genuinely looking for a relationship, and who doesn't want to waste your time with a self-serving arrangement that suits his convenience.

Chapter 20

Why Is a Good Man So Hard to Find?

Although in prior chapters I've explained how you might be contributing to your difficulties in getting the relationship you want, there's also another important factor to consider. That maybe good men are hard to find!

From my research I've found that many men are struggling with relationship issues that could eliminate them from the "good men" category.

Terry Real told me, "In three out four couples that I see in my practice, the man is grandiose." A high ratio, indeed.

He defines grandiosity as "a kind of empathy deficiency toward others. What is missing is a capacity to sufficiently cherish those around us."[1] In his book *How Can I Get Through to You, Closing the Gap Between Men and Women*, Real explains that he works with men who are grandiose by helping them regain sensitivity to their impact on the women they're involved with.[2] Real admits that he himself has struggled with his own grandiosity but has worked it through in psychotherapy! He even reports that he has a successful relationship with his wife.

Psychoanalyst and academic Janet Sayes also discusses men's grandiosity in her book *Boy Crazy*. She writes: "Researchers find that young men often idolize themselves, and grandiosely identify with the superlatives such figures represent. Asked to describe their actual and ideal self, men are more likely than women to deflate the two. They grandly describe themselves as though they were already their ideal selves. They are more likely to describe themselves in self-inflating terms. They reckon themselves to be more attractive than young women reckon themselves to be."[3] Putting grandiosity to the side, some experts, many of which are men, claim it's men's general psychological makeup that makes them so difficult to have relationships with.

Psychologist Dr. Herb Goldberg, author of *What Men Really Want*, writes: "The way men love and what they need in relationships are different and often the opposite of what women need. Indeed men's needs in relationships, for better or for worse, because of their condition as men, have been to suppress or deny vulnerability and personal needs to avoid losing control or getting too close."[4]

The world-renowned psychoanalyst and psychiatrist Dr. Otto Kernberg explains in his book, *Love Relations*, that "men and women are developmentally different and that the adult woman has potentially greater courage and capacity for a heterosexual commitment than the adult man." He also writes that "men have less capacity than women for establishing a dependent relationship."[5]

Even our old friend Terry Real has said, "The skills needed to tolerate strong emotions are both daunting and unfamiliar to many men."[6]

If men's psychological limitations that lead to poor relationship skills aren't enough of an obstacle to contend with, we are even challenged by our own brain chemistry. When we are lucky enough to finally find a "good man," we often automatically dismiss him or turn him away due to our genetic makeup. I was turned on to this concept by the renowned anthropologist and Rutgers professor Dr. Helen Fisher, who told me that women have been immensely attracted to very aggressive men with elevated testosterone levels for millions of years! She also claims that women have always gone for the macho, resourceful leader of the pack from the beginning of time! So, do we just naturally dig the primitive, brutal caveman? Despite all of our efforts, are our biological instincts causing us to seek out unavailable men?

One woman on my message board posted the following on a forum about women who are attracted to cops: "Women go nuts for cops. It's not just the uniform. The gun equals manhood & safety. It's testosterone in a holster. They're the ultimate 'Bad Boy' except they're 'safe' because they're law enforcement."

I decided to test my "bad boy" theory using a pop culture example. I chose the movie *In the Cut* about an English teacher (played by Meg Ryan) who falls for macho "bad boy" Terry Malloy, an aggressive, seductive detective (played by Mark Ruffalo). On the DVD version of the movie, Mark Ruffalo is interviewed and, interestingly enough, he appears to be the exact opposite of his character—down-to-earth, sensitive, kind, almost gentle.

I asked twenty women to watch Ruffalo in character as Terry Malloy the "bad boy" cop, and as himself in the DVD interview. The results: Fourteen out of the twenty women I interviewed were more attracted to Ruffalo as the aggressive "bad boy" cop than when he was being his sweet vulnerable self. These are certainly not hard-and-fast scientific facts, but the results show an interesting trend toward the bad boy.

Even Karen Horney, one of the first psychoanalysts and a colleague of Sigmund Freud, who was notorious for her beliefs in women's independence, was openly attracted to bad boys. In her research about Horney, Janet Sayers found that Horney had a self-confessed attraction to "brutal and rather forceful men."[7]

Is it all about testosterone or is it more? Helen Fisher explains that the arousal system in the brain wants to "win." So if we see something that is hard to get, we want it. She refers to this as "Frustration Attraction" and further explains that as the dopamine in our brain increases, it results in focused attention and increased energy. In other words, if a reward or something we want is delayed, the dopamine increases, making us more alert and focused on attaining it.

A bad boy's characteristics, which include distancing, unreliability, unpredictability, and of course grandiosity, create emotional barriers that lead to frustration and results in a woman's brain releasing lots of dopamine, which, in turn, makes her obsessive in her attempts to capture her unavailable man's heart.

Even members of the psychoanalytic community are jumping on the bandwagon about how hard it is to find available men. I was very happy to meet New York psychoanalyst Dr. Janet Lieberman at a woman's conference in New York, where she presented her breakthrough paper "Issues in the Psychoanalytic Treatment of Single Females Over Thirty." Lieberman explained that a woman's inability to marry is not necessarily due to her psychological issues, that perhaps some of the problems are sociological. She states in her paper:

Women reach their late twenties and increasingly as they get older, there is a scarcity of suitable men available to them. The shortage of heterosexual men capable of long commitment like marriage to women over thirty seems to be a fact of reality that is commonly overlooked or even denied by society. If the reports I hear are true, many analysts deny this fact as well. Dr. Person acknowledges this scarcity of men as one of the major problems that confronts women today, and contributes to the transformation of a perfectly healthy longing for love into kind of deadly preoccupation. The frequent female obsession with love is in part the result of a demographic imbalance with profound psychological ramifications; A much-quoted recent study by Bennett and Bloom conducted at Yale and Harvard, entitled "Why Fewer American Women Marry," reported that college educated women at thirty have only a 20 percent chance of marrying and those of thirty-five have a 5 percent chance. These statistics seem to be the result of number factors, including the greater longevity of women and social norms that permit men to marry women younger and less educated than themselves. Marrying younger women is considered to be a status symbol for middle- and upper-class men. Men find it acceptable to marry women who are intellectually, socially, and professionally beneath them, whereas women usually do not find such marriages acceptable. There may even be rise in the population of men who are overtly homosexual and of men who are unable to make commitments. Additionally, many men report that they are threatened by the recent advances women have made, both professionally and socially.[8]

Well, with all this bad news said and done, I can't help but disclose my own findings that, despite our brain chemistry, sociology, and men still lagging behind us in relationship skills, women still manage to find love and successful romantic attachment. If you read the women's sport's page (AKA *The New York Times* wedding section), you'll see that women of all ages are still getting married. Weddings are still very "in" and are, in fact, a billion-dollar business.

However, I will say that the women I have known through my psychotherapy practice and personal life who have succeeded in marrying or finding a successful and loving attachment with a man tend to have many of the following traits:

- They are less picky about superficial qualities such as washboard abs. (Yes, this was actually a criterion one woman said a man must have to date her. As of yet she still hasn't married.)
- They are more demanding about his characterological traits, which include stability, ability to attach, dependability, emotional availability, consistency, emotional supportiveness, and ability to follow through.
- They are willing to make more compromises in order to be partnered. For example, she may be willing to accept a man who earns less money than she does or is not as handsome as she hoped. This can be considered "settling" to some, but this is a relative and personal choice.
- They have an easier time letting go. Although they get just as upset as the next woman when a relationship doesn't work out, they don't obsess or ruminate as much about "the man who got away." They don't mourn as long or examine what went wrong to cause a romance with a man to turn sour. They say "next" easier.
- They are sometimes well networked and have a number of people to introduce them to men or take them to parties where they can meet men.
- They are goal-oriented toward meeting a man and finding a relationship. They do whatever it takes, including doing the personal ads, going to nightclubs or bars, asking to be introduced to men, going to charity events, etc.
- They tend to be proactive and resourceful, not just depending on running into a man through natural circumstances, although they are aware that this can also work.
- They have a very positive relationship with at least one parent

or caretaker. They've experienced being loved by someone who raised them, which they replicate in a relationship with a man.

- They often have good judgment when it comes to men and romance. They are good to talk to when you are having man problems.
- They are not ashamed of their longings for attachment, love, or marriage.
- They are very hopeful, despite the bad odds or obvious difficulties, that they will meet and connect with a man.
- They tend to stay away from men who are "marriage phobic," or "unavailable," "bad boys," and "men who are terrified of commitment and attachment."

So, although it can seem that you're swimming against the tide when you're trying to find a "good man," according to psychoanalyst Dr. Sue Kolod, "It's my belief, and I've been through this over and over again, when a woman becomes ready for a relationship she finds one."

Although I tend to agree with her, I still think a good man is hard to find.

Chapter 21

The Dating Cure's Twenty-Step Program

1. Look for Important Qualities You Want in a Man

He should be someone who is:

- Reliable
- Accountable
- Emotionally stable
- Able to relate to a person other than himself
- Attracted to and interested in you
- Trustworthy
- Sensitive
- Responsive to your needs
- Not addicted to drugs or alcohol
- Empathic
- Generous
- Caring
- Has good morals
- A good listener
- Not mysterious
- Capable of earning a living
- Physically and emotionally available
- Consistent
- Not a user

2. Be Observant

When you meet a man, observe how he behaves, reacts, communicates, and expresses his feelings. How a man behaves will give you clues to his personality. For instance, if he doesn't listen to you when you express your feelings, then he's not sympathetic or empathetic. Some men don't have a clue to the feelings they are experiencing, which will make it hard for you when you're both trying to communicate. If he doesn't call when he says he will, he's unreliable. So watch what he does. Action speaks louder than words. Don't be in denial.

3. Be Persistent

Trust and believe that you will find a man you can have a healthy relationship with. Many of the women I have known (including my clients) who wanted to hook up with a man almost always found someone. They had their minds made up and were very determined, despite the odds against them. Get ready to put a lot of energy into your search. It will take time and effort. It may not happen by chance. You have to get yourself out there. Market yourself. Tell your friends, acquaintances, and family members that you're interested in meeting a man. Not just any man, but a man who is available and emotionally healthy, with many of the qualities I listed earlier, and looking for a relationship. Ask them to introduce you. Do the personals. Go to nightclubs and bars with your friends. Go to all social events you get invited to. Network, network, network! I had a Grand-Aunt Bella who called looking for a man "going fishing"—so cast that net out there, ladies. No one said it was easy.

4. Don't Waste Precious Time

Once you see a man has severe intimacy and/or personality issues and is not a good prospect for a relationship, move on. Don't waste your precious, valuable time trying to fix him or wait for him to change. You are not his mama. Remember, the clock keeps ticking. Father Time waits for no one.

5. Be Socially Available

When looking for a relationship, it is a necessity to make sure you're available for dates. When you're initially looking to meet a new man, it's not the time to play hard-to-get. You must make socializing and going out a priority. When you get invited to a party or event, go. Don't be a couch potato.

6. Try Dating Outside the Box

Don't stay restricted to your same familiar prototype or blueprint. The less rigid you are about whom you are willing to date, the more men will be available for you to choose from.

7. Be Patient

As they say, patience is a virtue. Don't get crazy when you get disappointed. Hang in there! It takes time. More often than not, you have to kiss a lot of frogs to find your prince. I've known women to go on more than seventy blind dates until they met "the one."

8. Be Aware of How You Sabotage Relationships with Men

Read the chapters (Chapters 1 through 7) on the prototypes of women carefully. See if you fit into any of the categories. Try to work on any of your behaviors that are self-defeating or self-destructive to relationships with men.

9. Work on Yourself

In priming yourself for that special relationship, try the following:

- Increasing your self-awareness
- Increasing your self-esteem
- Increasing your internal self-regulation of your emotions
- Decreasing your self-destructive behaviors

10. Work on Not Acting Desperate

Here are a few tips you can try to help yourself from acting desperate:
- Stop obsessing
- Stop overanalyzing
- Stop wondering "what if I had done this, or done that . . ."
- Stop compulsively digging for answers
- Whatever you do, don't act clingy!

11. Work on Improving Your Judgment of Men

When looking for the right guy, you may need to adjust your own expectations of what he should be like. To size him up right, you should:
- Stop being naive
- Become sharper
- Trust your instincts
- Stop idealizing chemistry
- Learn from your mistakes rather than repeat your unproductive or self-defeating patterns

12. Try to Resolve Childhood Issues

Try to work through any issues from your childhood that are interfering with making good choices or affecting the way you relate to men.

13. Try to Resolve Past Issues with Men from Your Adulthood

Try to work through any trauma or wounds you have incurred since you have been an adult, such as breakups, abandonment, rape, violence, rejections, emotional or physical abuse, poverty, or discrimination. Utilize individual psychotherapy, support groups, twelve-step programs, books, and workshops to work through all past traumas.

14. Work on Your Support System

Build up a support system with friends, relatives, coworkers, and therapists who will be there for you when you're feeling anxious or panicky. Tell them that you are going through a period of meeting new men, which can be stressful, and you may need them for advice, reality testing, and encouragement, and to help you to contain your feelings of anxiety, disappointment, and even anger and frustration. Make sure you always have some of their phone numbers on hand. Rotate people in your support system so that one or two individuals don't get burned out. You certainly don't want them to feel used and exploited. Take the time to be there for people in your support system as well.

15. Don't Personalize Everything

When you're dating take what happens with a grain of salt. Often you don't really know the man well, so don't take what happens to heart. If he acts in any way rejecting, remember it's not always about you. He could be angry at his ex and displacing his feelings on to you, or he may be looking for a replica of his high school sweetheart. Who even knows what he's looking for. Some men are very fantasy-driven, on a quest for a woman who doesn't even exist. If you don't fit the bill as this perfect woman, he crosses you off the list, and you never hear from him again. Remember that dating is not always enjoyable but a necessary process to find the man you are searching for. So sometimes you have to be a bit business-like and thick skinned.

16. Never Be Afraid to Reinvent Yourself

There is nothing wrong with change and rediscovering who you are. Pour your creativity into you. You are your own lifetime project.

17. Know What's Going On Out There

Don't lock yourself into a certain set of behaviors or beliefs about men, love, and relationships. Listen with an open mind to what the experts are saying on the radio and TV or in newspapers and magazines. Become aware of the dating trends in our culture. For instance, it's now hip for older women to date younger men. Just look at Demi and Ashton!

18. Don't Be Afraid of Therapy

You can never have enough therapy. Emotional self-growth is endless. It's like peeling away layers of an onion. When things get too rough, don't be afraid or ashamed of seeing a therapist or joining a therapy group. Not only will it help pull you through a rough time, it may give you the wisdom you can use for a lifetime. Therapy can also help you improve your judgment and reality testing so you don't keep repeating the same mistakes over and over again.

19. Nurture Yourself

If you didn't get enough self-soothing as a child, now's the time to catch up. Nurture, nurture, nurture yourself. Men may come and go, but you're always stuck with you, so take care of you. As Whitney Houston says (she should listen to her own advice), loving yourself is "the greatest love of all."

20. Visualize Your "New" Ideal Man

Do visualizations of your ideal man every day. Based on the work you've done in this book, and using the good men in your life as role models, create the image of your ideal man, someone who is capable of a healthy, long-term relationship. Here's a sample list written by a member of the support group I run in New York City:

- Someone who is cultured (i.e., food, travel, art)
- Someone athletic/active
- Someone who has plenty of hair on his head
- Someone who is well mannered/chivalrous
- Someone who is ambitious
- Someone who is financially stable/well off
- Someone who is funny/playful
- Someone who is honest
- Someone who is loving
- Someone who is understanding

Now create your own list. List his qualities here:

1.

2.

3.

4.

5.

6.

7.

8.

9.

10.

Chapter 22

Last Thoughts from Rhonda

Dating nowadays often demands you to be a warrior! Especially when you're trying to find a man in the Internet age, when another woman is just a mouse click away. So as you date to find the man you're searching for, take your time and don't rush things. Instant relationships are not the solution. Unfortunately, there are no shortcuts. It's a universal truth that relationships need time to unfold. It takes a while for people to reveal themselves and to build trust. If dating gets too overwhelming, there's nothing wrong with taking a break. Being alone can be revitalizing.

Always hold on to your "true and real self" whether that means being with the man you're happy with despite others' opinions, staying single until you find your soul mate, or leaving a man because he's not meeting your needs.

If you do get rejected (a man doesn't call you back or want a relationship with you), don't dwell on him. Accept the negative experience, learn from it, and move on. Don't focus on a man who doesn't want you.

Although I've explained in *The Dating Cure* how you are responsible for your own behavior and thoughts, it's also important to remember that the universe, culture, and the men you meet have their own agendas—bear that in mind as you embark on your exciting but challenging dating journey.

Footnotes

Chapter 17: The Men You're Attracted To

1. Otto F. Kernberg, *Love Relations, Normality and Pathology* (New York: Yale University Press, 1995), p. 9.

Chapter 20: Why Is a Good Man So Hard to Find?

1. Terry Real, *How Can I Get Through to You?*, New York, Simon & Schuster, 2002), p. 132.
2. Real, p. 132.
3. Janet Sayers, (New York: Routledge, 1998), p. 118.
4. Herb Goldberg, *What Men Really Want* (New York: Signet Book, 1991), p. 20.
5. Kernberg, p. 84.
6. Real, p. 63.
7. Sayers, p. 127.
8. Janice S. Lieberman, "Issues in the Psychoanalytical Treatment of Single Female over Thirty," *Psychoanalytic Review*, 78, Summer 1991: 2.